D0802941

Good 'n' Angry

Good 'n' Angry

*How to Handle
Your Anger Positively*

Les Carter

Baker Book House
Grand Rapids, Michigan 49506

ISBN: cloth: 0-8010-2488-9
       paper: 0-8010-2481-1

Fourth printing, January 1987

Library of Congress Card Catalog Number: 82-73843
Printed in the United States of America

Unless otherwise indicated, Scripture references are from the New American
Standard Bible, ©The Lockman Foundation 1960, 1962, 1963, 1968, 1971,
1973, 1975, 1977.

Contents

Part Four
Getting Anger Under Control

Foreword

$\mathbb{D}$r. Les Carter has done it again. Dr. Carter has analyzed the two primary sources of emotional pain in his first two books. In *Why Be Lonely?*, he thoroughly addressed solutions to the pain of loneliness. In this book, *Good 'n' Angry*, Dr. Carter has dealt with the primary cause of most of our emotional pain: improper handling of the emotion of anger. As a psychiatrist I fully believe that the improper handling of anger causes about 95 percent of psychological depressions. I also am convinced that a fear of becoming aware of the anger we hold within ourselves is a primary cause of anxiety.

In this book Dr. Carter has done a better job of describing the causes and dynamics of anger-related emotional pain than has the author of any book or article I have ever read on the subject. His recommendations for getting anger under control are biblically accurate and psychologically sound. Christians and non-Christians alike will benefit by reading and applying the sound advice in this book. Christians in particular will benefit from this book because there has been so much unbiblical teaching within churches and seminars across America on the subject of handling anger. Well-intentioned Christian leaders have given damaging advice, which has resulted in thousands of unnecessary cases of clinical depression in America.

With this book Dr. Carter shows that people can be both good and angry. Christ Himself became very angry at times and yet was without sin. The Bible gives much advice on controlling that God-given emotion. This book is a must for every person who wants to minimize the emotional pain he will experience in this life.

Paul Meier
Associate Professor of
Pastoral Ministries
Dallas Theological Seminary

February 1982

Introduction

I was sitting in my den recently, reading through the newspaper, when I came upon the headline "Hostility on the Highways." I assumed this would be one of those cute semipsychological articles telling why people tailgate and blow their horns at each other. To my surprise it was a serious article that told how innocent people were taken from their cars and beaten by other motorists who had become impatient in traffic. I began wondering what this world is coming to.

I suppose we all have our moments when we lose our cool. It's not unusual to feel aggravated about being caught in snarled traffic. And we all have known moments of irritation with friends, acquaintances, and family members who do not live up to certain expectations. We can even say that it is harmless if a person becomes angry every now and then. But enough is enough.

There comes a time when anger can be very harmful. When it is allowed to flow uncontrolled, there is no limit to the destruction anger can cause. Every work day I listen to people in my counseling office tell about the emotional hang-ups they have carried through the years. Almost every person who has emotional problems can tell about times when anger was used inappropriately in his formative years. The result is that as these people grew to be adults, they knew that anger is potentially destructive, yet didn't know what to do with it when they felt it.

Most people seem to agree that the most satisfying lifestyle is one in which composure prevails. They will claim that they desire to practice patience and understanding in their relations with one another. But when they least need it or expect it, something happens to foul things up. Someone speaks in a manner they despise. An unexpected event disrupts their tightly packed schedule. They were counting on a friend to do a particular favor, but it never gets done. Someone reminds them of an embarrassing personal failure that supposedly was done and forgotten. One thing after another can happen to spoil a person's good intentions! Before you know it, anger breaks loose in a destructive expression.

Has this ever happened to you?

Do you know what it is like to give your emotional stability over to anger?

Of course you do. All of us, at one time or another, have let this emotion take charge in our lives in an unflattering way. It is humbling to admit that we are not always in control of ourselves in the way we know we are supposed to be.

We all know what uncontrolled anger can do to our interpersonal relationships. Just one angry moment can spoil hours, months, or even years of living with good intentions. Anger can cause gaps to form in once-solid relationships. It can cause some relationships to dissolve altogether. Uncontrolled anger has been instrumental in the breakup of families, friendships, and business associations. It can cause guilt complexes and inferiority feelings. It is usually the basis of depression and anxiety.

In short, it would be of great benefit if we could learn to maintain some control over this emotion in order to prevent disruption from prevailing in our lives. This does not mean that a person should get to the point where anger is never felt or expressed. That is neither humanly possible nor desirable. Anger per se is not wrong. It is the way we use and express it that can be labeled right or wrong.

"Good 'n' angry" is an old expression used to describe someone who is really upset. For example, a father might become good 'n' angry when his son leaves his power tools out in the rain. Or perhaps a schoolteacher might be good 'n' angry when the class is especially disruptive. I don't know how the expression was coined. Whenever most people are "good 'n' angry" they are usually very angry, but their behavior is not so good.

Let's hope that it is possible to be both angry and good at the same time. Anger is a normal part of being human. We are in deep trouble if every time we feel angry we wind up doing something disastrously wrong. Unfortunately, though, due to a poor understanding of anger, many people fall short of being both angry and good.

Think back to your earliest or most memorable experiences with anger. Were you taught that it was all right to have that emotion? Or were you made to feel that you were a bad person because of your emotion? More than likely, the latter was true. When they are growing up, children are usually taught, either subtly or openly, that anger is an emotion that should be avoided at all costs. If children become angry, they learn that they must be handling their problems poorly. As adults, they hold on to the concept learned in childhood: "Angry people are bad people."

We could rationalize that this teaching has been passed on for justifiable reasons. That is, for centuries, anger indeed has been mishandled by every breathing soul. It has been displayed in ridiculous, destructive behaviors. It has been abused by egomaniacs who were trying to meet their own selfish needs, or sly manipulators who have mistreated and belittled people due to their own unresolved conflicts.

Because anger has been (and still is) expressed inappropriately, it has been labeled as being negative. People assume it represents nothing good. It is supposed to be a sign of emotional instability or immaturity. But that is only part of the truth about anger.

My desire is that, by understanding anger, you can come to the point where your control of it is appropriate. I hope that in the process you will gain a greater understanding of yourself and of others. Perhaps you can even find some strength in your anger and learn to channel it in a positive way. By understanding how to control this emotion you can free yourself to live a life of caring and concern.

This book is divided into four sections. First is a description of what anger is and how people can identify it in their lives. Second is an explanation about why anger gets the best of us. You will be able to look at patterns of thinking and behaving that make anger an enemy. The third section looks at the way anger is expressed. We each have differing styles of letting our anger seep out. The fourth section maps out a strategy for putting together a lifestyle that allows for anger in a pattern of Christian love.

PART One

Know What Anger Is

1

To Be Or Not to Be

$\mathbb{B}$efore we get too far into our study on anger, it is best to point out that some people don't feel a need to keep anger under control. Some people enjoy being angry! These people recognize that with anger come certain "rewards," such as power, intimidation, emotional distance, and the ability to manipulate. While the average person might not see these traits as rewarding, some warped minds thrive on these fruits of anger.

Anger can be a lifestyle of choice. After all, God created each person with a free will. This means that people can control the direction they choose to follow in their personal lives. Anyone who lives a life of anger is *choosing* to do so. No one is holding a shotgun over him to force him to act angrily. These people are angry because they choose to be. One can always claim that we are all the products of our family environment. We can say that people are what their backgrounds have taught them to be. But that is only partially true. As adults, we have the capability to decide whether we will keep or weed out certain traits learned in our formative years. Clearly, we are what we choose to be.

I am assuming that most readers of this book are wanting to learn to have a better grip on their anger. But before you look at how to understand and control anger, it can be helpful to review some strategies a person can use to mold himself into a consistently angry person. By looking at this side of life, one might become more motivated to choose a lifestyle of relative calm. (Perhaps not, but that will be for you to decide.)

Following is a guaranteed formula on how to become a consistently angry person. If this formula is adhered to closely, there will be no doubt regarding your temperament.

1. Be picky and finicky. Take pride in being a perfectionist. Some of the angriest people in the world are perfectionists. After all, what thing is there that is perfect? Certainly nothing human is perfect. Therefore, people who expect perfection from others or from themselves are guaranteed to find frustration. The picky person wants each and every little thing to fit in its prescribed position. These people are idealists to the extreme. They have a beautiful, glossy picture of how the world should be, and they refuse to have happiness until all of their specifications are met. They frequently use words such as "have to," "should," and "must." Everything and everybody has its place and function. This person will angrily busy himself in trying desperately to make the world perfect.

2. Don't listen to another person's point of view. In discussions be concerned only with getting your own opinions across. One of the keys to being a consistently angry person is to be a poor listener. We all know that listening is a vital part of the communication process. If there is a steady flow of give and take in conversations, calmness and levelheadedness are likely to prevail. So if a person is dedicated to being angry, he won't allow any give and take. Instead, when others have a point to be made (particularly if *they* are angry), the dedicated hothead will react defensively. He will insist that no one else knows what he is talking about. He certainly won't entertain the thought that what others are saying might be valid. He

will have one and only one goal in his interactions. That is, he will not stop until he has completely expressed his opinions at least eight times. Who cares what other people have to say?

3. Hold on so firmly to your religious convictions that you can't help but condemn someone who disagrees with you. Most Christians have an assurance of one thing. They know they are correct in their beliefs. They have found the absolute truth. This must mean that anyone who has any other ideas must be wrong. Angry people will watch others living a lifestyle that they know to be wrong and, because they know those people are heathens, they will have scorn. Rather than feeling love and patience, the committed angry persons will be repulsed. They will want to have nothing to do with anyone else. Occasionally they might try to pound someone on the head with their Bibles in order to knock some sense into that person. But there will be no other contact.

4. Pride yourself on *never* being silly. That is, don't laugh and have a good time. Be serious. After all, once you learn the skill of being chronically able to be serious it is easy to find things to be angry about. The next time you are engaging in some light conversation, throw in some gloomy comments about the state of our economy. And if that doesn't dampen the mood, talk endlessly about the rising crime rate. With everything being so miserable, who can afford to smile? Angry people will think only of the dark side of life. They will worry about all those bills to be paid. They will want to discuss the spread of Communism or the increase in moral decay with anyone who will listen. If anyone tells a joke or a funny story, they will shake their heads in disgust over the frivolous attitude of the common folk. It's those silly people who don't concern themselves with all the burdens of the world who are making life's problems more complex.

5. Overload your schedule. We all know how leisure

time and relaxation can make for a calm disposition. Therefore, if people are striving toward a life of anger they can become workaholics. On the surface, these work-aholics may seem like nice, responsible people. But don't be fooled. People who load up their free time with one responsibility after another will sooner or later protest that they aren't getting their fair share out of life. They will frequently grumble about how other people are lazy and irresponsible. In fact, this can lead to a prevailing attitude of pessimism. Also, by being so busy, they will probably lose a lot of sleep. This can be an extra bonus, since anyone who does not get proper sleep is naturally going to become irritable.

6. Expect others to cater to your every whim. We may be taught in our churches that part of the Christian life includes learning to be loving and caring. You might go so far as to say that sounds nice. But don't do it—not if you are to succeed at having an angry disposition. Rather than trying to serve people and to make life pleasant for them, be selfish. Have high expectations for what other people can do for you. For example, if you are a man, proclaim yourself king of the castle. Constantly remind your family of the things they are expected to do to make life easy for you. Women, cry a lot when someone in your family makes a mistake or forgets to do the things you have asked. Whether by subtle manipulation or out-right demands, always remind others of their duties and obligations.

7. Constantly demand your rights. This is one of the surest steps to take toward a life of anger. Our newspapers are filled with accounts of one group after another that is demanding its rights. You might as well jump on the bandwagon, too. Forget that the Bible emphasizes re-sponsibilities rather than rights. Don't worry about that—demand your rights anyway. By being a rights activist you can let your selfish side come forth. If everyone in this

world would work at being responsible toward one another, we wouldn't have to demand rights. This means
that we also might not have much anger. But you can help
to create tension by joining with groups that are constantly criticizing other people who do not think the way
they do. Join several.

8. Make fun of things such as love and gentleness. Those
characteristics are for people in the Dark Ages. You
might as well face it, it's a competitive world out there.
This step can be particularly easy for men to do. After all,
our culture puts a premium on being tough. Gentle men
are looked upon as sissies. If your wife and children want
to go to church, let them go by themselves. Also, make it
clear that it is strictly a woman's duty to do the loving
things such as spending time with the children or buying
birthday cards for relatives. Concern yourself only with
real men's work and pride yourself on being tough.

9. Speak in a loud, booming voice when you have a point
to make. In fact, practice shouting. Common sense tells us
that speaking in a soft, caring voice will help create an
atmosphere of harmony. Since your goal is to create the
opposite, you will want to try to be intimidating in the
way you talk with people. In discussion, if other people
don't agree with you right away, yell at them. This is very
effective with family members. Not only does it create
tension, but it also teaches them through role modeling
how they should behave. By setting this type of example,
perhaps your children or spouse will imitate you. Think
of all the wild scenes this can create!

10. Worship money and material possessions. Make
them more important than human relations. If you are to
become an angry person you must get your priorities
right. As far as you are concerned, people are a means to
an end. They are meant to be used to get you all the riches
you desire. Once their usefulness is spent, leave them,
have nothing to do with them. Anger, as I am referring to

it here, is a self-centered emotion. Therefore, you want your desires and goals to be consistent. By being concerned primarily with what you will get from people, you are perpetuating the lifestyle that is best suited for anger.

11. Don't look at your personality to examine your strengths and weaknesses. If you are ever going to succeed at being a volcanic person, don't try to improve yourself. Anyone who looks seriously at his personality flaws might actually find ways to become more mature. This would work against your objectives. If someone gives you feedback about how you are behaving inappropriately, snarl at him and tell him to be quiet. By all means, don't read the Bible or listen to sermons. You might become convicted of your need to change. One way to keep from looking at your weaknesses is to simply deny that you have any.

12. Have no compassion for people who are suffering. You are a self-made person. You've picked yourself up by the bootstraps to make yourself what you are today. Everyone else should do the same. As far as you are concerned, there is no excuse for human frailty. It is all a cop-out for a bunch of lazy people who want things handed to them on a silver platter. Never mind that people may have had difficult circumstances to withstand in their formative years. Never mind that they may not have been encouraged to feel good about themselves. Life hasn't been a bed of roses for you, either. Those are just lame excuses for weaklings who are not willing to tough out life's problems the way you have.

13. Learn to nag and criticize. Look for the worst in people and focus on it. This step can be carried out only by someone who is a dedicated pessimist. For example, when you look at the problems of the world, just shake your head and mumble something about the sorry politicians who got us into this mess. When you see others making mistakes, point it out to them in a condescending

manner. Whatever you do, don't ever try to find ways that you can be of help in someone's trouble spots. That might ruin your image. Think only of how you can make people aware of their faults. If you don't point out problem areas, who will?

I call this formula for an angry lifestyle "Thirteen Steps to a Life of Misery." After carefully considering each of the steps, you may decide that this is the life for you. Actually, if you are already a skilled hothead you know that these steps only scratch the surface. You can use your own imagination to create many more characteristics that will fit the pattern, which can mold you into a living, walking volcano.

However, you may decide that a life of anger is not what you will choose for yourself. You may conclude that there are more productive ways to live your life. If that is the case, you are urged to continue reading. What you will find in the pages that follow will be explanations of why anger exists, how it tends to be manifested, and how a person can develop a lifestyle of even-temperedness and responsibility. The choice is yours.

2

Mirror, Mirror on the Wall

People who are willing to look closely at themselves in order to honestly evaluate their strengths and weaknesses are the ones who are most able to grow. In my counseling practice I have worked with countless angry people who did not know they were angry. Because of the sophistication of our language they were able to use all kinds of words to describe anger so that it didn't sound like anger! People say they are anxious, bored, depressed, or frustrated. They will say that they are anything but angry. These people are the ones who have a serious need to be very honest with themselves.

In order to start out with a good idea of how much anger you have, it would be helpful for you to complete this inventory. By determining your level of anger you can properly motivate yourself to find the appropriate remedies. Complete these questions as quickly as you can. Your first response is usually going to be the best.

1. I concern myself with others' opinions of me more than I like to admit.   T   F
2. It is not unusual for me to have a restless feeling on the inside.   T   F

3. I have had relationships with others that could be described as stormy or unstable.   T   F

4. It seems that I wind up helping others more than they help me.   T   F

5. I sometimes wonder how much my friends or family members accept me.   T   F

6. At times I seem to have an unusual amount of guilt even though it seems unnecessary.   T   F

7. At times I prefer to get away rather than to be around people.   T   F

8. I realize that I don't like to admit to myself how angry I feel.   T   F

9. Sometimes I use humor to avoid facing my feelings or to keep others from knowing how I really feel.   T   F

10. I have a problem of thinking too many critical thoughts.   T   F

11. Sometimes I can use sarcasm in a very biting way.   T   F

12. I have known moments of great tension and stress.   T   F

13. When I feel angry sometimes I find myself doing things I know are wrong.   T   F

14. I like having times when no one knows what I am doing.   T   F

15. I usually don't tell people when I feel hurt.   T   F

16. At times I wish I had more friends.   T   F

17. I find myself having many bodily aches and pains.   T   F

18. I have had trouble in the past in relating with members of the opposite sex.   T   F

19. Criticism bothers me a great deal.   T   F

20. I desire acceptance by others, but fear rejection.   T   F

21. I worry a lot about my relationships with others.   T   F

22. I believe I am somewhat socially withdrawn.   T   F

23. I believe I am overly sensitive to rejection.   T   F

24. I find myself preoccupied with my personal goals for success.   T   F

25. I often have felt inferior to others.   T   F

26. There are times when I like to convince myself that I am superior to others.   T   F

27. Even though I don't like it, I sometimes am phony in social settings.   T   F

28. I don't seem to have the emotional support I would like from my family or friends.   T   F

29. I'd like to tell people exactly what I think.   T   F

30. My concentration sometimes seems poor.   T   F

31. I have had sleep patterns that do not seem normal.   T   F

32. I worry about financial matters.   T   F

33. There are times when I feel inadequate in the way I handle personal relationships.   T   F

34. My conscience bothers me about things I have done in the past.   T   F

35. Sometimes it seems that my religious life is more of a burden than a help.   T   F

36. There are times when I would like to run away from home.   T   F

37. I have had too many quarrels or disagreements with members of my family.   T   F

38. I have been disillusioned with love.   T   F

39. Sometimes I have difficulty controlling my weight, whether gaining or losing too much.   T   F

40. At times I feel that life owes me more than it has given me.   T   F

41. I have had trouble controlling my sexual urges.   T   F

42. To be honest, I prefer to find someone to blame my problems on.   T   F

43. My greatest struggles are within myself.   T   F

44. Other people find more fault with me than they
    really should.   T   F

45. Many of the nice things I do are done out of a
    sense of obligation.   T   F

46. Many mornings I wake up not feeling refreshed.   T   F

47. I find myself saying things sometimes that I
    shouldn't have said.   T   F

48. It is not unusual for me to forget someone's name
    after I have just met him.   T   F

49. It is difficult for me to motivate myself to do
    things that don't have to be done.   T   F

50. My decisions are often governed by my feelings.   T   F

51. When something irritates me I find it hard to get
    calmed down quickly.   T   F

52. I would rather watch a good sporting event than
    spend a quiet evening at home.   T   F

53. I am hesitant for people to give me suggestions,
    even if they are positive.   T   F

54. I tend to speak out when someone wants to know
    my opinions.   T   F

55. I would rather entertain guests in my own home
    than be entertained by them.   T   F

56. When people are being unreasonable I usually
    take a strong dislike to them.   T   F

57. I am a fairly strict person, liking things to be
    done in a predictable way.   T   F

58. I consider myself to be possessive in my personal
    relationships.   T   F

59. Sometimes I could be described as moody.   T   F

60. People who know me well would say I am
    stubborn.   T   F

Now, go back and count the number of *T*'s you circled.
This will tell you how great your need is to confront your
anger.

If you scored less than 15, you probably have pretty

good control over your anger (or else you were using a lot of denial). Look back over the questions you responded to with a T and you will be able to focus on those items as areas for further improvement.

If you scored between 15 and 30, you are probably in the normal range. You are willing to admit that you have anger within you and you know you have plenty of room to grow. You will need to be careful as you better learn to handle your anger.

Those of you who scored between 31 and 40 probably have experienced more than your share of problems. Chances are you have had more dissatisfying moments than you would like to admit.

And those whose score is 41 or greater need to head for the nearest psychologist. You will have to work diligently at keeping your anger under control.

The truth is that we all know anger and we all have handled it at some time in an inappropriate manner. We each need to open our minds to find ways to live our lives as responsibly as possible.

3

Stand Up and Be Counted

There are many popular theories about what anger is and why it exists. Some experts state that anger is a reaction to repressed childhood experiences. Others say it is a frenzied style of crying out for love. Still others insist that it is the epitome of selfishness. To be honest, it is nearly impossible to say exactly what anger is. Most of the theories about anger are probably at least partially correct. But none is totally correct. One of the ways to understand this emotion is to look for the common thread that is found in each experience.

Stop for a moment and think of several instances when your anger has been aroused. As different as these experiences may be, there is virtually always something similar. When anger comes into people's lives, it is usually because they have felt unappreciated, belittled, taken for granted, helpless, or in someway insignificant. (The only exception is true righteous anger.) Anger is an emotional reaction that comes in the face of wrongdoing.

Perhaps you became angry when the coffee pot malfunctioned, burning out a fuse. You were in a hurry and it caused great inconvenience. In becoming angry, you were saying to that coffee pot, "Why in the world did you pick a time like this to break down? Can't you see that I have other things to do? This shouldn't have happened to me. I don't deserve mishaps like this!"

Maybe you can think of a time when your spouse forgot to do the special favor he had promised to do a week ago. You were irritated because his forgetfulness seems to be an indication that he did not place your needs very high on his list of priorities. Through anger you were probably communicating, "I'm tired of being taken for granted. If you *really* cared for me you would do what you said you would do. You must think that I'm not all that important around here. But I have news for you. I am someone to be reckoned with!"

By expressing the anger that they feel toward some one or some thing, most people are *standing up* for themselves. They are trying to drive home the idea that they deserve to be treated correctly. Whether they express anger toward a family member, a stranger on the street, or the next-door neighbor's dog, people are trying to express the conviction that they have some worth, and they want to be treated in a worthy manner. Sounds pretty simple, doesn't it?

Anger is a way of saying, "Notice my needs!" That's why it is usually expressed when a person feels ignored, put down, or unappreciated by another person (or persons). When something happens that does not affirm their worth as humans, people are prone to being angry. From the illustrations already given, it is evident that people can be made to feel insignificant even by inanimate objects. (Have you ever kicked a vending machine that has "eaten" your money and given you nothing in return?)

Admittedly, anger is not always rational. But rational or not, when anger is used as an emotion that "speaks up" for personal needs, it indicates some real strength. Most people are quick to recognize that there is a lot of strong (in the sense that it is intense) anger in this world. Many people have difficulty in understanding the positive nature of anger. But indeed, a person who feels anger is a person who is exhibiting something positive. You might ask, "How's that? How can we find anything positive about a person who yells or pouts or fumes about insignificant things? After all, anger can make people look very foolish."

Yes, anger can make people look foolish. But look at the basis of every incident where anger is involved. The angry person is *trying* to stand up for himself. He is *trying* to convince the world that he deserves to be treated with respect. Sometimes it is hard to find this positive element in anger when the anger is coming from someone who seriously abuses this emotion. But it can be found. In fact, it can be sad to know a person who never becomes angry because that person likely feels that he is too worthless to speak up for himself.

In my lifetime I have met quite a few men and women who have had serious trouble with the law. (My father was once a prison psychologist.) I've met people who range from the slick, high-powered crime-network organizer to the small-time street hoodlum. One man whom I particularly remember is Tom. Of his thirty-six years, eighteen had been spent behind bars. He was one of the meanest creatures to walk the earth. Though he had never been accused of murder (he probably just had never been caught), he had done almost everything else, from robbery to drug dealing to rape to smuggling. It was evident when anyone met this man that he had intense rage inside.

You might ask, "How can there be anything positive about the anger that boiled inside a person like Tom?" Certainly Tom's anger was exhibited in extremely irresponsible ways. But to understand his anger, it is helpful to look at the circumstances that led him into such a life. Tom had nothing good in his early family life. His mother was a weak woman who would make many idle threats to him, but of course she would never follow through. His dad was alcoholic, and when he was home he would beat Tom severely. Tom resented this treatment. Rather than giving in to such treatment, he decided that he would learn to fight back. Deep inside he believed that he did not deserve to be treated so wrongly. He developed a rough edge to his personality in order to protect himself. It was his belief that if he could be mean enough, people would show him respect.

Inside Tom was the need for a feeling of worth. He invested a great deal of energy into a lifestyle that would get him what he believed to be proper treatment from others. Of course, it is obvious that Tom channeled his energies in an entirely wrong direction. This is what led him into such a wretched lifestyle. But even though his behavior was horrendous, we can find that in the beginning, Tom *thought* he was doing something good for himself. His anger started out as a method of self-preservation, though it ended as a pattern of destruction.

The example of Tom teaches a delicate fact about anger. That is, we as human beings are capable of taking something positive and useful and turning it into something horrible. This is why many people try to avoid anger altogether. This explains why people balk when I talk with them about anger being a personal asset. What was originally given to mankind as a gift (the ability to stand up for oneself) by God has been sorely abused. The example of Tom represents the extreme, so let's look at a more typical situation.

Carolyn was prone to periods of anger. She was a respected professional woman who had grown up in a normal middle-American household. She married her long-time sweetheart and was expected to live happily ever after. But Carolyn seemed to have one problem that got in the way of her pursuit of happiness. That problem was her husband, James. James always seemed to do things the wrong way. He was constantly making mistakes (in Carolyn's eyes) and exhibiting annoying habits. (Actually he just had a few minor quirks.) She would fuss at him and correct him constantly. In anger she would criticize him and let him know how disappointed she was. Even when he would try to please her it would never be good enough, and she would become more irate.

On the surface, it's hard to find anything positive about Carolyn's behavior. After all, she was helping to ruin her marriage by her constant nagging and criticism. But the fact remains, Carolyn was exhibiting an inner strength; unfortunately, she was showing this strength in a negative manner. We might compare her anger to a muscleman who uses his power to tear apart useful objects. By showing anger, Carolyn was attempting to communicate that her husband should give her more consideration. She felt insulted because he did not live his life the way she wanted him to. So, in anger, she set out to get what she felt was necessary for herself. Her original intentions to have a good marriage were fine. She just went about achieving her goal in the wrong way.

In the purest sense, there is nothing wrong with taking care of one's personal needs. This is what Carolyn thought she was doing. But this trait can easily become something negative because of selfishness. Carolyn was acting in behalf of herself, but she apparently felt no regard for the responsibility she had as a wife. Her anger originally began as a positive characteristic, but it ended up backfiring. Her husband felt the need to defend himself, so he, too, developed feelings of anger. It's sad to realize that people often fail to think before they express their emotions. Humans can be extremely impulsive.

But, thank goodness, not all anger is used in this selfish way. Anger can be constructive. For example, Jason was an eight-year-old newcomer to his school. Because he was the new kid in class, several of the boys decided to test him. They would hide his books and tease him unmercifully on the playground. Finally Jason had enough. He pulled the ringleader aside and convincingly told this boy that he had had enough of the others' antics. It was time to put an end to their tricks and insults. The children were convinced that Jason was serious, and they respected him for standing up to the class troublemaker. They decided to change their ways and stop their tomfoolery. Once the problem was over, Jason quickly dropped his anger.

In this illustration, anger was used appropriately. Jason did not resort to any of the dirty tricks that often accompany anger. (He had been well coached by his parents.) Rather, he simply used anger to let the other children know that he was someone of value and he wished to be treated as such.

The difference between Jason's and Carolyn's use of anger is glaring. Both felt mistreated, and both were standing up for themselves. In Jason's case he truly was being treated wrongly. Carolyn was being finicky and was making issues of minor differences. Once Jason expressed his anger, he dropped it. When Carolyn felt anger, she held on to it for hours and hours at a time. Jason simply had a conviction that he wanted to be treated fairly by his peers. Carolyn wanted more. She wanted superiority and power.

Selfishness is the single trait that has given anger a bad name. Most people spend far too much time worrying about themselves. They automatically become agitated when they feel cheated in their relationships. They believe that imperfect circumstances should be eliminated totally from their lives. So they strike out in anger. It is as though the world has the responsibility of living according to their own personal standards. Because of selfishness, people can take a positive trait (standing up for oneself) and turn it into a monster.

As you seek to find a proper way to be angry, you will want to be careful to avoid extremes. Unlike Tom and Carolyn, you want to avoid the hostile extreme by accepting responsibility *before* showing anger. And you want to be sure to avoid the extreme that says anger is never to be expressed. For when something irritating happens, no one is doing himself a favor by becoming passive and taking the martyr's approach. Imagine the emotional stability of the person who says, "Oh, well, I've just been insulted by my best friend. And my kids are getting into all kinds of trouble. I'd better not get angry. I'm afraid I might offend someone. Besides, I don't deserve to speak up. I'm not worth much anyway." This is just as irresponsible as explosive anger.

This book is seeking to explain a middle-of-the-road approach to anger, an approach that is realistic and responsible. The basic assumption is that anger is not all bad. It is born of a sense of self-preservation. In our imperfection we are capable of abusing anger by taking it beyond its intended purpose and using it for purely selfish gain. Some people will need to learn to use anger less frequently, others more powerfully.

4

The Two Types of Anger

Anger per se is neither good nor bad. It is how people use their anger that makes it positive or negative. Ideally, anger was given to humans by God as a tool to help build relationships. In its pure form, anger is an emotional signal that tells a person something needs to be changed. It was intended to be a positive motivator to be used in giving one another feedback about how life can be lived more productively.

I can recall many times in my life when I needed to be reprimanded. One particular incident sticks out in my mind. As a six-year-old boy I once witnessed an older boy breaking out a window of a neighbor's house with a rock. He laughed about it and seemed to enjoy it, so I thought I would have a good time, too. I got a handful of rocks and went behind the same neighbor's house to his garage and proceeded to break all the windows in his garage. It seemed like great fun. However, as you might have guessed, I was caught by my father, who didn't share the same enthusiasm with me. On the contrary, he was quite angry. Here I was breaking the windows of a good friend's garage! Naturally I was punished and had to pay the neighbor for the damage. In addition, I received a well-remembered explanation about the wrongness of my actions.

What would have happened to me if no one had become angry with my childish deeds of irresponsibility? A good guess is that I would have become worse. Today I might have a resemblance to the apostle Paul—that is, I could be writing to you from a prison cell. The anger my father exhibited was proper because it taught me a principle about correct living. If he had just snickered and said, "Boys will be boys," I would have learned to continue my wrong behavior. His anger was proper in that it had positive results.

If my father had beaten me unmercifully and had made a public spectacle of me, his anger would have been destructive. Not only would I not have felt sorry for what I did, but I also would have had a sense of vengeance. I would have vowed that next time I just wouldn't get caught. An overuse of anger can lead to serious repercussions.

There are two types of anger, assertive and aggressive. In the last ten years or so, much has been written and said about assertive anger. I think some people have overstated its usefulness. In its pure sense, however, assertiveness means to put forward one's beliefs and values in a confident, self-assured manner. When used correctly, assertiveness is a positive trait. Certainly each person faces many situations that go against his most basic beliefs. By being assertive, he demonstrates a sense of strong commitment to what he knows is right. This is the type of anger that the Bible encourages us to use. It is the only type of anger used by Jesus Christ.

Aggressive anger, on the other hand, goes too far. Like assertiveness, aggressive anger seeks to put forward one's beliefs about what one believes to be right. However, aggressive anger is used in an abrasive, insensitive way. Assertive anger is helpful and is careful to consider another person's welfare; aggressiveness is inconsiderate. When people use an aggressive style of anger, there is little concern for the impact the anger will have on the recipient. There is little empathy involved. Consequently, aggressive anger tends to be destructive. People need to examine aggressive anger closely because, unfortunately, most tend to use this type of anger much more frequently than they do assertive anger. Aggressiveness is a direct reflection of the sin nature that exists within a person.

Jeanne had a great deal of aggressiveness inside herself. She could make a convincing argument about why she had every reason to be angry. She had been married for nine years to a man who wasn't ever going to be nominated by anyone as Husband of the Year. The truth is, her husband, Tim, did not take good care of himself physically; he was overweight and unkempt-looking. He drank too much and spent too much time away from home. He did little to help with household chores or with taking care of the children. No doubt Jeanne had plenty of reasons to be angry. Her husband needed to hear her feedback.

But rather than working with Tim in a constructive manner, Jeanne used her anger destructively. She only added to the problems with her wrath. When Tim would drink too heavily, she would nag at him endlessly and tell him how worthless he was. When he did not discipline the children correctly, she told him how he was ruining their lives (as if she were the perfect mother). When they had one of their rare moments of calm she would talk in pessimistic tones of how their marriage would never work. She tried to make Tim feel guilty so that he would be motivated to change.

It doesn't take a psychologist to figure out that this type of angry abuse is not going to help matters. It is only going to make a bad situation worse. Jeanne seemingly had proper goals in mind when she expressed this aggressive anger. She wanted her husband to do his share toward making the marriage work. But her use of anger was so abrasive that she got the opposite of what she said she wanted.

The thing that sets aggressive anger apart from assertive anger is its destructiveness. Most of the anger expressed by the average person has destructive consequences. Usually we get so wrapped up in trying to correct something we believe to be wrong that we get carried away. We do not make the effort to apply solid, constructive communication in those situations. Notice the differences between aggressive and assertive anger.

Aggressive Anger	Assertive Anger
Seeks to punish a person who does wrong.	Seeks to help a person who does wrong.
Does not care about the other person's point of view.	Tries to be understanding.
Is stubborn, immovable, and demanding.	Is flexible and willing to seek alternatives.
Is condemning and judgmental.	Recognizes we all have faults.
Has high expectations of everyone.	Knows that even the finest people sometimes make mistakes.
Cares about what happens to oneself.	Cares about the welfare of others.
Holds grudges.	Knows the value of forgiving.
Does not notice one's own areas of weaknesses.	Recognizes that one can always improve.

I mentioned that aggressive anger is a reflection of the sin nature of man. All people, even Christians, have a battle raging within themselves. Like our earthly parents, Adam and Eve, all people have made choices that they know to be wrong. The Scripture insists that regardless of our church backgrounds we all know right from wrong: "Ever since the creation of the world his invisible nature, namely, his eternal power and deity, has been clearly perceived in the things that have been made. So they are without excuse" (Rom. 1:20, RSV).

God created everyone with an inborn knowledge of Him. No one can state that he doesn't know the nature of God, because all men are aware of who He is. This means all people also have an inborn sense of right and wrong. (Anthropologists have found that even the most primitive tribes have rules that closely resemble biblical guidelines.) But in spite of our innate knowledge of God, people insist, like Adam and Eve, on doing as they please. The sin nature has one basic objective: Look out for oneself.

This is why each person is capable of using a positive gift, such as anger, for his own selfish desires. Even though anger was given as a tool to build relationships, we use it for our own selfish gain. Consequently, it winds up working in negative ways. We can compare anger to a tool, the crowbar. A crowbar has many useful functions. It can be used to pry open boxes or windows that are stuck shut. It can be used to pull nails out of wood. It can be used as a lever to lift heavy objects. In short, the crowbar was invented as a handy helper. But a crowbar can also be used for wrong purposes. It can be used to break into someone's house. It can be used as a lethal weapon. It can be used to break up objects of value. In other words, a crowbar's worth depends solely on the motivations of the person using it. There is no limit to its constructive or destructive use, except for how the user handles it.

If people allow their sin nature to control their lives, there is no limit to the destructiveness they can become involved in. If they want, they can take a simple emotion such as anger and turn it into a demonic force. Of if they want to, they can use anger as an instrument of love and growth. Once people understand the dual nature of this emotion, they likely will be very careful in the way that they use it. It is frightening to imagine the impact this one emotion can have on our lives.

PART Two

Why Anger Gets Out of Hand

5

I'm Depending on You!

Every human being alive is dependent on someone or something. A wife may depend on her husband to make the money to keep the family budget afloat. A child depends on parents to make him feel loved and secure. Even a hermit depends on people to leave him alone. Part of human nature is to look to other people to help give us the things we want and need in life. This is a normal trait.

However, there is a problem with being dependent. Other people are not always dependable. They are imperfect, and sometimes insensitive to others' needs. This means that there are going to be times when we will feel let down. We'll be disappointed. As long as people are mortal, mistake-making human beings, we will not fulfill one another's needs in a perfect way. This is a fact that all of us can accept intellectually, but we have a hard time accepting it emotionally. For example, I may be able to say that I know my wife has weaknesses, but when her weaknesses surface, I can become angry. Emotionally I would not be accepting what I know intellectually. When this happens, my dependent nature is being overactive.

Most people who have a strong temper consider themselves to be anything but dependent. They proudly proclaim how independent their lifestyle is. They may point to the fact that they are self-starters; they like to get things done; they consider themselves to be decisive, not wishy-washy. Rules are made to be questioned. When asked to describe themselves they may come up with terms such as "individualist," "stubborn," or "nonconformist."

But these traits do not necessarily mean that a person is truly independent, at least not in the emotional sense. While these people may appear to be independent, inwardly there is a strong dependence on other people. In Texas (where I live) there are many high-powered, wealthy men in oil-related businesses. One particular executive seems to exude power. He will be seen driving only his big, black, expensive car. He wears suits made by the finest custom tailors in town. He smokes two-dollar cigars. And he speaks in a loud, booming voice. He is the type of person who "won't take no for an answer." Whatever he wants, somehow he gets. This executive seems extremely independent. But in getting to know him, I learned that all of the show that he puts on in public is just a phony game. Deep inside, he hungered for approval. As a boy, he did not feel accepted by his father and mother. He began looking for ways to make people notice him. Just by knowing this little bit about this man, any amateur psychologist could figure out why he chose to put on such an act. He was depending on other peoples' approval to make him feel worthwhile.

In counseling sessions, when I first talk with angry people about their dependent nature, they usually deny that this is a problem for them. Like the high-powered oil executive, they see themselves in such puffed-up terms that they cannot admit that they want approval from others. But usually after further discussion, they come to admit that the desire for approval truly is a deep problem and a key factor in their anger.

If persons are truly independent emotionally, then why would they have an angry flare-up whenever situations are not to their liking? By nature an independent person is able to maintain emotional control in the midst of trying circumstances. He would be rational in the midst of irrationality, moderate rather than extreme, levelheaded rather than volatile.

Notice what an angry person is trying to communicate. Through anger he is saying, "I am not going to feel satisfied until you behave to my liking," or, "I will continue to be upset if you don't change your attitude." In other words, the angry person is depending on someone else to make changes before he will get his own emotions under control. He is allowing outer circumstances to control his inner feelings. He will not become emotionally stable until external factors fall into place. Since no one can count on having these circumstances fit the perfect game plan, the person who continues in this kind of anger is guaranteeing only personal heartbreak.

Those people who continually struggle with anger are not using their personal abilities to take charge of their own emotions. They become reactors rather than initiators. They are letting unpredictable circumstances have control. These people, rather than having a firm grip on their own anger, are gripped by anger. Some of these people may actually insult themselves by saying, "I just can't control my anger; it is too powerful." They are assuming that they are too weak to take charge of their own lives. This is a cop-out.

Joan was a young woman who did not outwardly express her anger very often. But she had quite a bit of anger bottled up inside. Rather than saying she was angry, she simply referred to herself as being "a little frustrated." She assumed that she was doomed to a life of frustration because of the imperfection she had to face every day. For example, she didn't like having to plan her daily schedule around the activities of her children. Her husband had annoying habits such as being late or being lazy. She had little patience when she went to her women's meetings only to find that the leaders were long-winded and boring. Her friends seemed to be wrapped up in their own soap-opera-type lives, which she found unamusing. In short, one instance after another caused Joan's stomach to churn. She seemed to go from one frustrating circumstance to another, never finding anything to her complete liking.

Clearly, Joan's problem was that she reacted to the people around her. When something came up that she did not like she would automatically respond in frustration. She would allow her frustration to take control of her inner self. It could ruin her happy moods and it could break her sense of concentration. In short, Joan was depending heavily on the people around her to behave in a manner that would allow her to be calm. If the circumstances did not meet her approval, she was locked into her angry feelings because she would not draw upon her inner strength to give herself the stability she wanted.

Realistically, it is naive to believe that a person can have total emotional independence. In fact, it is not even desirable to be completely independent. Remember, dependency is a normal trait. Our goal is to avoid being extreme. That is, we want to avoid latching on like leeches to others and we also want to avoid being totally aloof. Each of us is wisest to strive for *moderate* dependency.

Notice how we have a built-in need to depend on one another. In earliest infancy, a person is totally dependent. An infant depends on Mom and Dad for food, clothing, cleaning, and protection. Most of all, the infant depends on parents for love. (Long ago, researchers found that some infants who died in orphanages had all of their physical needs met, but died from a lack of consistent love from a dependable parent figure.) As infants grow, they learn to spend time away from Mom and Dad and to feel secure in doing things on their own. And of course, by the time they become adults, they ideally should be prepared to meet the dependency needs of the next generation.

But no one ever completely outgrows this inborn sense of dependency. No one ever becomes so smug that he loses the desire to feel loved. (Some people lose hope of feeling loved, but that's a different story.) As normal adults they certainly do not need another person to dress them or to spoon feed them their meals. That would be absurd. Yet adults still depend on one another for deeper, inner needs. We all want to know that someone values us. In fact, we can go so far as to say that this dependency is a God-given gift intended to be used to draw people to one another in love.

It is certainly necessary for people, as creations of God, to recognize their dependence upon Him. He is the one who grants life. He gives meaning to life. People get their sense of worth from Him. He is the one who has deemed all people lovable. When people recognize their own failures and inadequacies they know that they can always turn to Him to give them guidance and strength. The problem is that people do not always understand God and use Him as He would have them do. Instead of looking to Him for strength, people tend to look to one another. The more a person comes to depend on the love of God, the more steady his emotions will be. The more that person seeks the favor of imperfect humans, the more prone he will be to anger. The tendency is to forget the real God and make gods out of people. Some individuals make people's opinions of them more important than God's.

So it is no crime to admit that all people have dependency needs. People are dependent on one another, and are dependent upon God to make them feel worthwhile. Dependency, in its positive sense, holds relationships together. But we humans seem to have an uncanny knack for taking a normal characteristic and twisting it out of shape. There are many who need to be aware of how they are capable of channeling their needs into inappropriate behaviors. How do angry people develop an improper sense of dependency? It usually goes back to the patterns a person learned as a child. Children can learn to have unnecessary feelings. Let's look at a few of the ways this can happen.

Feeling Unaccepted

I have already mentioned that one of the basic needs we all have is the need for love and a feeling of worth. Look at the way we all choose our friends. There are obvious factors, such as compatibility or availability, to consider in choosing a friend. But there will always be one factor in choosing a friend that is more important than any other. That is, we will want to know and feel that our friends like us. To put it another way, we want our friends to accept us just as we are.

It is when this need for acceptance is not adequately met that people feel the greatest anger. Rejection is something anyone has difficulty learning to handle, no matter how frequently or infrequently it occurs. If a person senses that he has lost the acceptance of another person, his natural tendency is to react angrily, as though he deserves something better.

Steve was a teen-ager who had a very critical mother. Day after day she pointed out his weaknesses and reminded him of how he needed her to make his decisions for him. She let him know that it was unacceptable to make mistakes. He was constantly scolded for petty things. Needless to say, Steve grew up with a poor self-image and a lot of self-doubt. He became the type of person who would do whatever his peers dared him to do, even if it went against his morals. He was desperate for acceptance.

In a counseling session, Steve stated that he did not

understand why he felt such violent rage toward people. As we explored his needs, he discovered that he felt that no one accepted him. It turned out that he had been programed to feel that way at home. His anger was his way of proclaiming his dismay about not being accepted!

Unfortunately, each person, like Steve, has felt a lack of perfect acceptance from others at some times in his life. Because ours is an imperfect world, people will always face the possibility of being treated unfairly. Sad as it may seem, it is true that no one ever will be completely accepted as he wishes. The chronically angry person is refusing to believe that anyone could possibly reject him. Intellectually he knows the world is imperfect, but he is hoping (even demanding) against all odds that he will receive far less than his share of rejection.

Feeling Controlled

Each year, as a child grows, it is normal for him to want to do things that make him feel more "grown up" or independent. The growing child feels he is increasingly capable to make more and more responsible decisions. His thought process and ability to reason become more refined. However, many children find that their timetable for becoming independent usually does not fully coincide with the parents' timetable. This is especially true in the teen years. As a result a power struggle erupts. There are arguments over how much self-control a child is allowed to exercise.

Many people have gone through their childhood years wishing that their parents and other authority figures would not be so controlling. They come to resent it when structure is placed on them. They complain of feeling trapped. They express a desire for increased personal freedom. During these years resentment can build toward anyone who imposes rules and limits.

Luther came from what was supposed to be an ideal home. His father had a respectable job and was in leadership positions in the church. His mother was very outgoing and involved in women's groups. They lived in a good neighborhood in a beautiful house. It seemed as though he had everything going for him. In fact, Luther had the reputation of being one of those guys a mother would want her daughter to go out with.

But Luther had a problem with anger. He was short-tempered and carried grudges against his family. His problem stemmed from the fact that his parents wanted (almost forced) him to project a clean-cut, all-American image. They emphasized that they wanted him to always stay out of trouble and to always set a good example. They placed strict limits on his social life as a way of "helping" him keep a squeaky-clean lifestyle. Their intentions were certainly honorable, but there was one problem. Luther felt forced into being what his parents said he should be. He actually agreed with most of the lessons his parents had tried to teach him. What he resented was that he was given no choice in how he would act. He was simply told what to do, and no questions were tolerated. As an adult, Luther had a hard time fitting into his work environment. He felt resentful everytime he was given a deadline. It reminded him of the all-or-nothing style of talk his parents had given him. When he married and started a family he was a poor husband. He saw marriage as a trap. To him it was nothing more than one obligation after another. Luther's problem stemmed from the fact that he had felt controlled and stymied as a teen-ager. He was determined as an adult to never let anyone tell him what to do or obligate him to fit any mold. No matter the cost, he was going to be his own person.

As you can see, feelings of rebellion and resentment are not restricted to teen-agers. If left unchecked, this pattern can continue indefinitely into adulthood. People often feel insulted when they are asked to submit to another person who is making demands. In fact, the anger can be more intense in adults because they have become accustomed to having freedom.

When people allow anger to indwell them in controlled situations, they are subconsciously communicating, "I am depending on that person to do what I want him to do so I can be happy. I cannot control my angry feelings until my external circumstances change to my liking." Whether the anger is explosive or silent, there is a dependency on external factors to give the angry person the emotional stability he desires.

Being Spoiled

We all are familiar with the stereotyped image of the spoiled rich kid. This child is the worst kind of brat because he is always accustomed to getting his way. When someone comes along who does not cater to him, he throws a temper tantrum. It seems that no one is consistent in telling him no. In a case like this, it is easy to show that the little fellow is depending on people to give him everything he wants—and then some.

Most normal people do not readily relate to the "rich-kid syndrome." But there are many people who have been spoiled in other ways. At counseling clinics across the land, the counselors' schedules are full with people who pout and become angry or depressed whenever they do not get their way. On the surface, these people usually have good reasons for being angry. It may be that a wife is complaining because her husband is not what she wants him to be. Or perhaps a single person is disillusioned by the competitive nature of the working world. More often than not, though, we find that the root problem is not those who are being "unfair" to these people. Rather, the problem lies with the ones who are accustomed to getting

their way and who do not know what to do when someone
doesn't act exactly as they wish.

If they are honest, most people will admit that it is
human nature to want to receive rather than to give. For
example, people often choose their friends or marriage
partners solely for what they will get. (Some people will
claim that their life is spent in one giving act after
another, but even in their giving they are expecting something
in return.) While it is normal to desire some of the
good things life can offer, many people often come to
expect and depend on those things before they can be
content.

The marriage relationship is the best example of how
people can be spoiled, only to become angry and disillusioned later when the royal treatment is not continued.
During courtship the man is usually on his best behavior.
After all, he is trying to impress his girl. He remembers
to open doors for his girl friend, he takes her to amusing
places, he dresses up for her, and he tries to dazzle her
with his witty conversation. In turn, the lady goes to great
lengths to please him. She puts on make-up and dresses
nicely. She cooks special meals for him. She even laughs
at his jokes when they are not funny.

The letdown often comes a few months into the marriage when they begin to take one another for granted
and see each other as they really are. The husband may
forget to compliment her. The wife may not cook as many
gourmet meals as she did before their marriage. Their
conversations are dull and tend to drag. For whatever
reason, the romance may dwindle. It is when this happens
that the couple had better watch out. Anger can result.
Couples will use phrases such as, "You never used to . . ."
or "Why don't we ever do . . . anymore?" The angry couple
may realize that they had become dependent on the royal
treatment and had not taken enough time to get to know
one another in the more mundane lifestyle.

This description of a spoiled marriage is only one example. Single adults may feel angry because they may not have that special someone to give them the care and the love they feel they deserve. Workers may become angry if they are not given proper treatment by fellow employees or superiors. Friends may break ties with one another over minor squabbles that are childish in nature. People who want (or expect) to be spoiled are setting themselves up for bouts with rage and hostility, since it is a guarantee that no one will cater to them in the exact manner that they want.

Being Selfish

The people who put their own personal needs ahead of others' needs are similar to the spoiled child. In fact, they are often one and the same. It is a simple truth that we all have selfishness in us. That is basically what the sin nature is all about. A person who spends any time at all observing the behaviors of a three-year-old will get a graphic illustration of what selfishness is like. Three-year-olds, innocent as they may be, assume that the world is supposed to revolve around them. If they do not get their way, they pout and squawk. If they get what they want they are content. It is as simple as that.

Ideally, adults will be able to put aside the blatant selfishness of a child and learn the art of sharing and being loving. But no matter how far a person goes in the maturing process, a remnant of that selfishness will remain. In some adults there is more than just a remnant. Many are as openly selfish as a three-year-old.

An old story tells of the best way to catch a monkey in the jungle. You take a hollowed-out gourd and put some choice nuts and berries inside. Leave a hole in the gourd that is barely big enough for the monkey to squeeze its paw through. Tie the gourd to a tree limb and wait. Soon a monkey will notice the gourd that holds the tempting goodies. The monkey will reach inside the gourd and fill its fist with the food. However, with its fist clenched, it won't be able to pull its paw out of the gourd because the opening is too small. Rather than dropping the food and slipping its paw out, the monkey will hold on tightly to its captured goods. It will jump up and down and go into a screaming rage, but will not let go of the food. Since the gourd is tied to a tree limb, the hunter can simply walk behind the monkey and capture it. The monkey will never know how it happened.

So often humans are captured by their emotions in much the same way. They may have their minds stubbornly set on getting the things that they selfishly desire in life. They become so intent on that one goal that they become oblivious to their pattern of self-destruction. An example is marriage partners who try so feverishly to make their spouse cater to their needs that they do not realize how their demands are destroying the marriage.

There is a difference between behavior that is purely selfish and behavior that aims to take care of oneself. People who are taking care of their needs are simply equipping themselves appropriately so they can function properly with others. A small example of this is the person who tries to get about eight hours of sleep each night. By being well rested he is able to carry on with personal responsibilities. Selfishness, on the other hand, is exemplified by the ones who don't care about the needs of other people. They are interested in personal gain. These people just make monkeys of themselves.

When people have this selfish attitude, it is clear that their dependent nature is overacting. The selfish person is worried about what he is going to get out of other people. "Are people going to respect me? Are my rights going to be violated? Will I get my slice of the pie?" Selfish people are depending on others' actions to give them emotional stability. This is a dangerous position to be in, since selfish people's mental stability is given over to people who are just as imperfect as they are.

Feeling Ignored

One of the worst feelings a person can have is to feel that no one truly notices him or cares about him. Our world is one that is fast-paced and highly materialistic. People's feelings seem to take a back seat to all the high-pressured problems of the world. Because of this, some people get the feeling that they don't count. Other things have higher priority to their friends and loved ones.

In my counseling practice, I have seen countless people who have had a history of feeling ignored by their parents, spouse, friends, or coworkers, and sometimes all of these. They have gotten the message that these people have so many more important things on their minds that they have precious little time to spend with one individual. They feel lost in the shuffle. Our world has come to embrace the idea that success means achievement in worldly pursuits, whether it be finances, grades, or being president of the women's club. This is opposed to the idea that success means consistent commitment to Christian living and meaningful human relationships.

I have already discussed the importance of feeling loved and accepted by someone significant. That significant person is usually a spouse, a parent, a child, or a close friend. When a person goes through life feeling consistently ignored by these people there is naturally going to be an emotional reaction. No one can belittle another person for feeling sad or hurt because of the persistent lack of love from significant people in one's life.

Do you see where the dependent nature is at work in this pattern? While it is understandable that a person feels hurt when he is ignored, it is counterproductive to convince oneself that life is meaningless until a specific person pays attention and makes him feel worthwhile. This is where rational thinking gives way to irrational thoughts. This makes fertile grounds for anger and bitterness to grow. Once again, it can be pointed out that it is a risky business to depend on someone else to make a person feel good. There are absolutely no guarantees that anyone can be depended on for all one's needs. Yet there are countless chances for this dependency to backfire.

Let's go back and emphasize one thought. It is not advisable for people to try to become emotionally independent to the extent that they become numb to the world around them. This is neither desirable nor even possible. Neither should people try to convince themselves that they don't need anyone else to give them pleasure in life. Rather, the goal is to try to learn to avoid thinking and living in the extreme ways that have been discussed in this chapter. Each person has inborn dependency needs. Yet each one also has the capability to let those needs become so exaggerated that he is controlled by them. What is needed in each person is to acknowledge his needs and then resolve to keep them in check so that emotions remain in proper balance.

6

Out from Under the Heap

History gives one example after another of people who overcame seemingly impossible odds to rise to prominence. There was once a six-year-old boy whom teachers considered to be backward and unteachable. This boy had difficulty with his vocabulary skills and was far behind the other children in simple tasks such as counting numbers. His teachers and parents alike feared that he would always be slower mentally than other children his age. His name was Albert Einstein.

Other great men have had to overcome many personal obstacles that ordinarily would classify them as second-rate. Abraham Lincoln was known for his moods of despair in which he would have serious doubts about his leadership abilities. Winston Churchill acknowledged that he was taken over periodically by depression and low self-confidence. Martin Luther had such turmoil inside himself that he feared that he was in danger of entering the gates of hell. These men whom history has recorded as being among the greatest who ever lived each struggled with a common foe—feelings of inferiority.

Whether we like to admit it or not, each of us spends time fighting off feelings of inferiority during the course of life. All people have occasions when they wonder about their true value and worth, when they feel inadequate. Some are successful at overcoming these feelings. Others are not. With some this struggle is glaringly obvious. With others it is quite subtle.

Inferiority feelings are defined as feelings of insignificance and worthlessness. They come at a time when a person degrades himself unnecessarily, and they are usually accompanied by feelings of guilt. These feelings of inferiority have a direct relationship to anger. After all, no one truly enjoys the distinction of being worthless. Everyone likes to think that he is as good as the next person. In fact, people are so conscious of their standing among others that they are prone to striking out at anyone who looks down upon them. Consequently, humans have developed a lifestyle of trying to impress one another in order to avoid the label *inferior.*

How do inferiority feelings develop? Certainly God did not create people to be inferior. We know that when God made man He saw that he was "very good." Unfortunately, many humans have misused their God-given skills to the point that each new generation is brought up to assume the position of inferiority. At the moment a newborn infant enters the world, he is totally lacking in survival skills. An infant literally is unable to do anything of a helpful manner for himself and for those around him. Of course, as the child grows older he begins to learn responsibilities and to become more of a "team member." Yet for years and years the child continues to get the message that there are millions of people (called adults) who can do things in a far superior way. A child can learn to be overwhelmed by the "greatness" of adults.

For example, a small child knows that if he cannot

open a jar of jelly, there is some strong, powerful person (usually Mom or Dad) who possesses the superior strength needed to do the job. In school a child learns that there are smart people and there are slow ones. Children are taught that if they ever want to be somebody, they had better become one of the ones on top. Failure is an ironclad indication of inferiority. Teen-agers are firmly convinced that if they are ever going to amount to anything they must be included in the "in" group. Among teen-agers there is a definite struggle for superiority and a dread of being deemed "out of it."

These are but a few of the common examples of how people can develop feelings of inferiority. Some people, though, have much more direct "lessons" in inferiority. Many people have been told repeatedly throughout their lives that they would never amount to anything. Others have never been allowed to make a significant decision for themselves. This, of course, reinforces the notion of being incompetent. Still others have been scolded for having hurt feelings or for making mistakes. They learn that only the "no-goods" show weaknesses.

Certainly the inferiority-superiority struggle is not limited to childhood experiences. Adults may be a little more sophisticated, but they still play the game. For example, mothers who have well-behaved, intelligent children may consider themselves to be superior to others. The businessman who makes $15,000 per year may be convinced that he is less worthy than the one who makes $100,000. The couple with a highly successful marriage may be seen as having an edge over those who have experienced divorce. I could go on and on, listing ways in which the superiority-inferiority game is played. But let's conclude that it is a problem all people know.

Built within each and every person is an aversion to feelings of inferiority. No one in his right mind looks forward to being treated as worthless. This simply is not natural. The Bible teaches that we are all created in the image of God (Gen. 1:26). In part, this means that each person has value and worth. (That is why God chose to send His Son to take the punishment for our sins. He believes we are *that* valuable.) This explains why people cringe at the thought of being labeled inferior. Deep inside there is an inner knowledge that affirms a sense of personal value. Because of this inborn sense of worth, people will react negatively whenever they are improperly condemned or criticized. This is the root cause for anger. Anger is a way of trying to refute the label *inferior.*

I don't worry nearly as much about the person who has chronic angry outbursts as I do about the person who allows people to constantly put him down. At the very least, the angry person still has enough get-up-and-go to defend himself, even if he does so inappropriately. He still has something inside to work with and to be correctly rechanneled. The passive person who never shows anger is giving up on himself. His passivity is his way of agreeing that he truly is inferior.

It is normal, even healthy, for people to have an emotional reaction when inferiority sets in. However, problems come when they overreact. Remember, the emotion, anger, is not necessarily right or wrong. It is how it is used that determines if it is right or wrong. As humans, we *need* to be willing to hold firm convictions and to speak up for what we know is correct. Unfortunately, some people use this self-preserving mechanism in an offensive way. Instead of using their inner resources to ward off inferior feelings, they use their inner energy to try to make themselves appear superior. Striving for superiority is not the solution to overcoming inferiority. Unfortunately, many people subconsciously decide that if they can appear to be top dog, it will prove that they are not inferior.

As a simple example, I will admit that I do not enjoy being criticized. Realistically, I know that in order to mature I can use plenty of constructive criticism. However, too much criticism can make me question my worth. It can make me feel inferior. Therefore, if someone heaps criticism upon me, my first tendency is to want to strike back. I will want to discover something about that person to embarrass him. Or perhaps I will want to use my wit to make that person look foolish. When this happens, I am actually trying to establish my superiority.

The problem with this style of fighting back is that it does nothing to resolve the problem. Just as there is no inferior human being, so there is no superior human being. Therefore, whenever anyone tries to establish himself as superior, it only makes matters worse. This keeps human relationships moving in a see-saw motion. The person who feels down tries to pump himself up. But in the process he puts others down, so they will seek to strike back. It can be a never-ending game of one-upmanship.

The way to handle feelings of inferiority is extremely simple (in theory). People need to remind themselves over and over that no matter what another person says or does, they are not inferior. Even when they make serious mistakes, they are not inferior. "Inferior" is a manmade notion. The only one who can deem someone as being inferior is God, and He does no such thing. He tells us that we are sinners and that we are rebellious, but never in His Word is there the thought that a person becomes worthless because of his weaknesses. We all are needy, yet we all are highly prized. When people concentrate on this concept of God's consistent love for every person, it erases the need to fight back when a misinformed human being proclaims that we are inferior. A person can have self-respect even in the face of shortcomings. If God says I am worth everything He has, who am I to refute Him?

People who forget to accept the acceptance given to

them by God become easy targets for the inferiority-superiority struggle. Either they will sink low into feelings of worthlessness or they will constantly live in ways that "prove" their toughness. Either way spells trouble. It is helpful to be able to examine your behavior patterns in order to find your areas of strength and weakness. Following is a list of behaviors likely in a person who gives in to the sense of worthlessness.

1. Depression sets in when someone loses his temper or is insulting to you.
2. You are afraid to speak up when a family member forgets to do that favor he promised to do.
3. Being a parent is a chore because it is so difficult for you.
4. When you do not get your way, you pout and sulk.
5. You are sensitive to criticism and feel hurt even when someone has a legitimate complaint against you.
6. You are afraid to say no.
7. You are reluctant to ask for something you want or deserve for fear of being turned down.
8. You don't want anyone to know your strengths, because to them your strengths may still be weak.
9. You would rather spend an evening alone than to be with a group of friends.
10. You have a quitter's attitude toward life. That is, you have given up hope for improving your circumstances.

People who have given in to the feeling of inferiority are looking at life with a narrow perspective. They assume that God's love and His promises are just empty words. They assume that because they have weak parts, all is bad. To them, there is only one way to handle the pain of feeling worthless—to quit. At least by quitting the struggle won't be so bad.

Mary had a lifestyle in which she seemed to be constantly reminded of her inferiority. She had an older sister who could do no wrong. In comparison, Mary was second-rate. When her parents divorced, there was a fight over who would have custody of her sister, but no one seemed to care about Mary. She stayed with her mother, but only because her mother felt a sense of duty. As an adult, Mary married a man who was "perfect." She assumed he would be the salvation she needed so desperately. He was successful in everything he tried. However, this created a problem for Mary, because she constantly felt insignificant in the shadow of her husband's achievements. His success reinforced her childhood feelings of inferiority. Mary's reaction to the worthlessness she felt inside was to be timid and chronically depressed. She assumed that it was her fate in life to be a second-rate person.

Mary's problem was that she did not recognize her inborn ability to pick herself up and create a positive, successful lifestyle. She felt uncomfortable with her inferiority, but not to the point that it pushed her forward. She knew the facts about God's love and unconditional acceptance, but those facts just didn't seem to apply to her. She needed to use some anger to enable her to confront the situation that caused her to feel lowly.

While there are some people, like Mary, who need to give themselves permission to be angry, there are others who overreact to their problems by trying to be superior. These people use anger destructively and fairly frequently. An example is Pam. Pam had felt put down all her life. Like Mary, she came from a broken home where she felt unwanted. However, rather than giving in to feelings of worthlessness, she became a fighter. If anyone dared to speak down to her, Pam was always ready with a strong comeback. One could describe her as being almost combative. She felt proud of her scrappy nature, since she knew she was taking the challenge of making something of herself with no outside help. The problem was that in the process of fighting for her own emotional survival, Pam was being highly inconsiderate of others' feelings. If they didn't like her style, she didn't care. She developed a cocky, superior attitude.

It is good to want to take care of one's own needs. But too often this is done in an abrasive manner. When a person tries to overcome feelings of inferiority by acting superior to others, he is only creating more problems. In order to get a good idea of how this works, examine the following guidelines for living a life of false superiority.

1. When someone is angry with you and insults you, yell back at him. Throw in a few condescending words of your own.
2. When you feel cheated, complain and grumble about how no one cares for you.
3. When someone confronts you about your weaknesses, give him the silent treatment. That'll show him.
4. Deny that you have any problems, even if they are glaringly obvious. Don't admit anything.
5. If you think that someone might try to take advantage of you, play the "poor me" game.
6. When you feel left out, complain loudly. Remind everyone of how rude they are.
7. Have a critical nature. If you put other people down first, that will give you the upper hand.
8. Talk behind people's backs. As long as you can make someone else look bad, you can assure yourself that you will look better in comparison.
9. If you are afraid to confront someone directly, use sarcasm.
10. Anytime someone tries to pin you down with a complaint (whether it is legitimate or not), make excuses.

11. Hold grudges and don't forgive until the other person agrees to a comprehensive list of conditions determined by you.

It should be obvious by looking over this list of "superior" behaviors that this type of lifestyle leads to emptiness. It is no more correct than a life of chronically feeling inferior. In one pattern anger is used too often and too destructively. In the other pattern, anger is used either too sparingly or in a passive, manipulative style. In either case, the individual is not facing his feelings head-on in a mature manner.

In order to break the grip of feelings of inferiority, it is important to have a correct self-image. Anyone who considers himself to be a worm is just as wrong as the person who considers himself to be God's gift to the world. In some Christian circles, people are taught to look upon themselves as lowly sinners undeserving of the love of God. While technically this is true, the idea is usually carried too far. Some people cite the passage in Romans 7 where Paul discusses the constant struggle with his sin nature. In the passage, he explains agonizingly how he does wrong things even though he has every intention to do right. He even makes the statement: "Wretched man that I am!" (v. 24). Some Christians will point to this and proclaim that if the great Christian, Paul, had this struggle, surely we all must consider ourselves wretched.

But it is not correct to build concepts on one or two isolated passages or a verse here and a verse there. We need to look at the entire message of the Scripture. In fact, in the same section where Paul tells the Romans of his wretchedness, he also makes a bold statement of his value and acceptance as a Christian: "There is therefore now no condemnation for those who are in Christ Jesus" (Rom. 8:1). Even though he had all kinds of weaknesses, Paul could feel relieved because God still loved him as

much as ever, thanks to the saving action of Jesus Christ.
Even though he had inferior feelings and behaviors, he
still was considered a lovable child of God.

As a person allows himself to become absorbed in the
enormous love of God, he will find an amazing lack of
worry about the world's judgments of him. The more we
allow God to love us, the more we will see ourselves as
being creatures of great value. While our human nature
is full of flaws, our inborn worth to God never changes.
What makes this concept so hard to grasp is that most of
us are accustomed to the judgments of human beings, and
we know how irrational they can be. Every person has a
desperate need to know and appreciate himself on God's
terms.

7

Because I Said So!

Most angry people have been called stubborn and unyielding at some time or another. The truth is that most of them *are* stubborn and unyielding. They have a way of thinking that is set in cement and they will not budge from it. Flexibility is not a strong suit with these people. In fact, many will insist that flexibility indicates weakness.

There is nothing wrong with having strong opinions. Actually it is very good for each of us to have a firm system of beliefs to guide us in our day-to-day living. In a world where there are too many wishy-washy people who will go along with the crowd, it is refreshing to find people who will say what they think. They do not feel compelled to always agree and say yes when they feel like saying no. No doubt, a well thought-out, complete set of values and opinions can be a great asset.

But too often people become so stubborn and defensive in their ways of thinking and behaving that they are obnoxious and hard to live with. As far as they are concerned, issues are either black or white. There is no gray area. Compromise is out!

This might work if ours were a totally black-and-white world. But it isn't. Our world is one that calls for a sense of give and take. Empathy and understanding for others are necessary tools in building human relationships. Anyone who refuses to acknowledge this is only trying to delude himself.

Because we live in a world in which issues aren't always clear-cut, people are going to be better off if they learn to adjust their thinking to it. That is, flexibility can become an asset rather than a sign of weakness. Does this mean that everyone should learn to settle for mediocrity and be willing to compromise at every turn? Not at all. It simply means we need to live by the basic rule: Be realistic.

A good example of people who lived with this rigid, stubborn thinking is the Pharisees of biblical days. In His earthly ministry, Jesus had a tremendous popular appeal to the common folk who were willing to admit their humanness. But the Pharisees were different. They were so holy and pious that they didn't need to listen to Jesus. They had their own customs that worked just fine for them, so they didn't want anyone coming along to rock the boat. They refused to listen to anything Jesus had to offer. These men always had an opinion about everything. And they were always right. (You now the type?) How frustrating to deal with people like this!

Today many people read about the Pharisees' haughtiness and say, "I'm glad I'm not like that." Yet many of these same people act haughty when they get angry. They insist that they have the answers for another person's problems. They refuse to listen to any point of view different from their own. They stubbornly repeat the same phrases and ideas without thinking them through.

For a long time Christians have had the reputation of being stubborn and inflexible. Why? Part of the reason lies in the way many of them present themselves to the public. They say they know the ultimate truths about the meaning of life, and they act huffy if anyone disagrees.

Their feelings are hurt if anyone dares to challenge them. They condemn those who commit sins they know they would never commit. They come across as being too angry!

Before anyone labels me as a wishy-washy Christian, let me assure you that I am fully aware of Jesus' anger. When He witnessed injustice it angered Him. He would speak His opinions with the highest authority. But His primary mission was not to show anger and to beat people over the head with His message. His mission was to show love.

Sometimes people get so caught up in forcing others to see things their way that they overdo. As I said, it is fine and proper to have strong convictions. The problem is not in having convictions, but in imposing those convictions upon other people. Angry people are so locked into the thought that things must be done in a specified way that they cannot cope when anything else occurs.

Angry people use some key words that identify them as controlling, authoritarian persons. Watch for the words *have to, must, ought to, should, had better, supposed to,* and *got to.* When people use these words excessively, it is a sure sign that they would like to have strong control over their environment. These people are the ones who are most prone to using aggressive anger.

Children would be the first to point out (if they were so bold) that we adults like to speak in authoritarian terms. Here is an example of an interchange that has infuriated many a child:

P: "Junior, we're having company tonight. I'd like for you to help clean up the house!"

C: "But, Mom, I've already made other plans. Why can't I help when I get back?"

P: "Because I said so, that's why!"

Mom had a specific objective in mind and things were going to be done exactly the way she said, no questions asked. Understanding and listening to what the child had to say was not an option. "Because I said so" was all the reasoning she needed. Perhaps the child had something legitimate to say, but we'll never know.

This heavy-handed style of handling children is needed only occasionally. But some parents use it constantly. It is the only style of relating they know. All adults were once children, so we all know how demeaning and discouraging this "have-to" style of interacting can be. It is very confining. Yet even though we know how aggravating it is to be on the receiving end of such brashness, we seem to be willing to dish it out to others when the chance comes.

Behind this heavy-handed communication there is a hidden expectation for perfection. The communicator is sending the message that there is one way, and only one way, for things to be done. Look at the perfection that is demanded everytime the have-to's are used in interchanges. For example, a wife might feel trapped by a husband who insists that she has to have dinner on the table by six o'clock. A child may feel great pressure from parents who tell him he has to do well in school. A mother may feel used when she feels she has to take her children on six errands in one day. When the have-to's become a part of life, it is virtually guaranteed that anger will erupt somewhere.

One example was Ellen. She was in her early forties and the mother of four children ranging from preschool age to high-school age. Ellen claimed she never felt that she had a life of her own. Her husband was a firm, stern man who had very specific expectations for the way Ellen should handle her responsibilities. She felt little freedom to be herself around him. In addition, the children constantly were in need of her "taxi service." She complained that there were days when it seemed as though she lived in the car. Her family life was very confining. What made matters worse was that Ellen had grown up in a very strict family. She had always been a good girl because she was afraid of the punishment she would receive if she ever misbehaved. Her entire life was dominated by the demands made upon her by other people. Ellen's reaction was to collapse in deep depression. She had repressed her anger to the extent that it finally got the best of her.

Living under authoritarian rule is bound to cause problems. Most Americans would agree that political authoritarian rule is certainly undesirable. Yet there are millions of individuals who in their private lives are authoritarian toward the ones they love most. It doesn't make sense! In the following sections we will take a brief glimpse of some of these persons and how they use their rigidness to annoy other people.

Mr. Big

Mr. Big always has had one goal in his life. He wants power, and lots of it. He grew up feeling awed by people who had authority, and he vowed that one day he too would work to get into a position that would demand respect and allegiance. He has developed many little characteristics designed to make people fear him. To enhance his image, he maintains an air of aloofness. That is, he does not say a friendly hello to people or recognize their presence unless he feels like it. He drives a big car and smokes a fat cigar, and you won't see him in anything but the finest clothes.

Mr. Big has few, if any, close friends. But he has plenty of underlings who "hop to" when he gives the word. Because he has such a need for power, he becomes very angry if anyone ever questions him or suggests that he is wrong. Mr. Big is never wrong. It is simply understood

that people are to do what he wishes and stay out of his
way unless he asks for them.

Of course, Mr. Big continues this pattern in his home
life. His wife, like all women, is little more than a glorified
maid. He makes no attempt to be understanding with her
or his children. The children are afraid of him. They know
that if they do anything wrong he will make their mother
punish them. Mr. Big may live out his entire adult life
without having a truly intimate conversation. He is seemingly content to know that others are in awe of him and
will cater to him.

The Moralist

The moralist is a person who has strong beliefs, usually
strong religious beliefs, that he assumes everyone should
have. If someone believes differently from him they are
like the lepers of old times; they are unclean and should
never be touched. When the moralist reads his Bible, he
does not see the parts that speak of the worth of the individual. He sees rules. He sees condemnation. He lives his
life in an effort to avoid God's punishment.

The moralist can be spotted a mile away. He seems very
friendly and eager to be of service to people. He has a
smug grin on his face. And, indeed, he may be the first to
volunteer when help is needed. But when it comes to
helping people with emotional needs the only thing he can
think to do is to quote Scriptures and give pat answers.
Every problem can be solved if a person will simply do all
the right things. He is well-intentioned in his dealings
with people, but he comes across as preachy.

The moralist does not understand why he does not have
any true close friends. He is not aware that people want
more than pat answers. He is woefully inadequate at
expressing feelings and becomes uncomfortable when

others show theirs. It surprises him when he learns that people don't like him. He is unaware of how he pushes people away with his powerful convictions. He may be very accurate in the facts he believes. But he lacks the personal dimension to put those facts together with a loving acceptance of human weaknesses.

The Pleader

Rather than telling people how things should or should not be done, the pleader begs. This person holds on to the hope that if only people would live in harmony (translated: agree in everything) then the world could be a perfect place. To her (most pleaders are women) there is a specific way that people ought to live: her way. She dedicates her daily energies to begging people to see the correctness of her way of life.

The pleader is not as imposing as Mr. Big or as condescending as the moralist, but she can be just as annoying, if not more so. She is especially skilled at using guilt to coerce people into living the way she wants them to. When she feels she might lose an argument, she will readily resort to the tactic of mentioning the ugly traits of her opponent. Or she will pout and look hurt, gaining sympathy with a broken expression or maybe a few tears.

The pleader will not take no for an answer. She is relentless in her pursuit of people whom she feels need to change. At the base of her personality is a deep lack of trust in people. Perhaps her personal needs have not been met by those closest to her. Perhaps she was openly abused as a child. Or perhaps she was spoiled as a child. Whatever the cause, there is no peace within this person until she has her way with people. Imagine the explosion she is capable of when she is rejected strongly enough by someone!

Miss Fussy

Miss Fussy is a perfectionist. She has her house arranged in perfect order. Miss Fussy loves to have company. She enjoys primping and making people feel right at home. The problem is that she worries so much about making people feel right at home that no one ever feels right at home around her.

Miss Fussy is eager to do things for people. But in spite of the fact that she seems so nice, her motives are questionable. The truth is, she doesn't trust people. Like others mentioned so far in this chapter, she has very rigid ways in which things must be done. She is constantly worrying that if she ever depends on anyone else, that person will let her down. Her motto is: "If you want something done right, do it yourself." Usually her anger does not come out in violent explosions. She is too proper for that. Rather, she is constantly riddled by minor irritations.

The Drill Sergeant

We all know one main thing about drill sergeants: They won't "take any lip" from anyone. This style of command may be fine for people who have just enlisted in the Marines and need whipping into shape. But what about at home, work, or other normal settings? Unfortunately, there are thousands of self-appointed drill sergeants who feel the need to pound their opinions and habits into others.

At home, the drill sergeant treats his family members as though they were machines. (Machines don't have emotions; they just perform functions.) The family comes to expect to be ordered around by him whenever he is home. "Please" is a word that is absent from his vocabulary. In his opinion, everyone has to work to prove his worth. If others cannot find something constructive to do, he will find it for them. When he makes family decisions, the only options considered are his.

If there are emotional problems to be solved, the drill sergeant has the answer: "Quit being a baby." His idea of tenderness is to give his wife some money so she can buy the children a little something. He will never admit that he has a weakness. Therefore, since he is able to conquer "silly emotions," so can everyone else. The truth is, he is so afraid of being close (vulnerable) to people that he feels a deep need to keep everyone at a distance. His gruff and bossy nature gives him the steel wall that he can hide behind.

The Martyr

The martyr is someone who does not give herself permission to say no. Unlike the other characters in this chapter, she does not impose her have-to's on other people. She imposes them on herself. She feels she must perform all the tasks requested of her or else she will be a truly bad person.

The martyr allows anyone and everyone to push her around and tell her what to do. Whether a committee chairman calls and asks her to do a job or whether a four-year-old girl insists on having her way, the martyr feels obliged to perform. She has many feelings she would like to express, but she is afraid of the rejection that might come. The troubling thing is that she finds herself in one compromising position after another. She feels used and unappreciated. But she does not dare to say anything. She is *supposed* to be a perfect wife, a perfect mother, a perfect friend. To show "negative" feelings would ruin her.

There are times when the martyr tells herself that she ought to be "selfish" and do things for herself. But she is convinced that if she were to stand up for herself, everyone would leave her. Besides, her sense of duty would not permit this. She is in a prison guarded by a wall of "should."

Each of these personality types is prone to anger. Though they may differ in their styles of relating to people, one common thread binds them all together. Each has a rigid system of beliefs that he or she falls back on because of his or her fear of being open with people. The have-to thinking saves these people from dealing with emotions. Their insecurity is so great that they do not know how to respond appropriately to something that is less than perfect. They are upset if their world does not follow the precise pattern they have imagined in their minds. Anger is their way of keeping the status quo.

People who live with these personality types also are prone to anger. As we have seen, each of these characters can be hard to put up with. We all may know certain truths about forgiving people for their faults and accepting their imperfections. But putting those truths into action takes discipline, lots of discipline. The recipients of the have-to's are called on to be just as careful in handling their own anger as are the characters who present the problems.

8

On the Treadmill

Ours is a culture that places heavy emphasis on how well people perform. People are constantly judging one another regarding their successes and achievements, or lack of them. Every time we turn around we are faced with the thought that people might label us as good or bad, nice or mean, excellent or poor. Consequently, people are prone to having emotional reactions when they feel they have been judged wrongly by someone.

This insistence on labeling one another creates more problems with guilt (again). Guilt has been so overused in our interactions with one another that it is a major reason that anger gets out of hand. Most people tend to look merely at outward achievements rather than inner motivations. Therefore, if someone does wrong, he is made to feel inferior.

A quick examination of the things that people consider important will illustrate how preoccupied we are with performance. For example, most people are impressed, even awed, by a person who has accumulated large sums of money. Without questioning that person's heart, they automatically judge the rich person as a success. And many people are equally hasty to label another person a failure if he has a mundane job that pays less than average wages. Forget that the executive has a bleeding ulcer and a poor family life. Forget that the worker has a heart of gold and a desire to be kind. The executive is automatically considered more important because of his performance.

As another example, perhaps some are impressed by the person with a quick wit who keeps people laughing and relaxed. A person who tends to be reserved and quiet is considered a dullard. Nine times out of ten the witty chap will receive more social praise than the quiet man, simply because people are impressed with outer appearances.

Many people who have emotional problems automatically assume they are bad or irresponsible because they have been taught that problems come only to weaklings. They assume that a good person is one who has it all together. Therefore, depressed people must be bad. Someone who breaks the law is despised. A divorcee is a reject. Having angry feelings means one is ugly. Only bad parents make mistakes.

Most people will acknowledge that just because a person performs poorly or makes mistakes does not mean he is automatically worthless. Nor is it true that a person who makes few visible mistakes is better than others. Most know that none of us has any right to judge another's character. Yet we do it constantly. Judgments seem to be such a part of our lives that we can't seem to help it. People make snap judgments before they realize what they are doing.

No one likes being on the receiving end of someone else's negative judgment. Most people cringe at the thought of doing something that will cause another person to shake his finger in disgust. Some people are so sensitive about being judged that they explode in anger when they sense someone is looking unfavorably on them. Many of these people simply lose their composure each time they detect a judgmental attitude from others.

Simply put, people resent being pigeonholed. They feel it is unfair to have to live up to certain criteria in order to be deemed acceptable. It gives them the same exhausting feeling that a person has when running on a treadmill. No matter how well they live, no matter how much they achieve, there is always more to accomplish. There are always more people to impress. It is a never-ending race. How frustrating! How angering this can be!

Closely related to the need to perform is the obsession our culture has for external appearances. The advertising world has skillfully picked up on the neurotic need to feel and look successful. Advertisers tell us that the "in" crowd is supposed to have the brightest teeth, shiniest hair, most aromatic fragrance. To be glamorous we are supposed to drive either a sports car or a sleek luxury car. It is all part of the game called "being impressive."

Even with our friends we continue the game. We know we are caught up in the game when we judge our neighbors according to how well manicured their lawns are. Men drool over beauty queens while hardly paying any attention to plain Janes. Women idolize their favorite movie stars and dream of being leading lady to Robert Redford. In short, we are deeply concerned with external beauty. Our judgments of people are superficial.

It Starts at Home

This pattern of striving for the praise of others has its roots in the way a person is reared. All children are exposed to judgments and evaluations based strictly on external performance. When a child shows Mom a drawing he made at school, notice her automatic response: "That's good. You've done a pretty job." When Junior brings home an *A* on his report card he is praised for his work. A grade of *D* will prompt a lengthy discussion about how he can bring his performance up to standard.

If two children are caught fighting, they are chided for their behavior and lectured on how to act properly.

There is nothing wrong with discussing performance with a child. Children need to learn how to act in a responsible manner. They need to learn how to put forth their best effort. But with most children, this is *all* that is discussed. It is rare to find grown-ups who will also discuss the child's feelings. Performances are highlighted; feelings are ignored. This is a subtle way for a child to learn that feelings don't matter. The child learns to perform well, but only so he will stay out of trouble. His first priority is to be accepted by authority figures. He learns to feel guilty if he does not fulfill all the conditions laid down by grown-ups.

With this extreme pressure to perform for acceptance, a sense of bitterness can slowly build inside of the individual. He begins to feel that he is not really accepted for who he is. He is accepted only for what he does. As adults, these individuals may unconsciously continue to perform and achieve in order to earn acceptance from others. But these same people often surprise themselves when they release inappropriate amounts of anger. By looking at this overall pattern of being "on stage," they could discover that their anger is actually a means of rebelling against people who tend to accept or reject them for external reasons.

True Guilt and False Guilt

One way to break the pattern of anger is to have a better understanding of guilt. Guilt is the feeling of shame that comes over people when they feel as though they have been wrong. It is accompanied by the judgment *bad*. The truth is, all people are guilty for one reason or another. That is, we all have done things we know are wrong.

But there are two kinds of guilt: true guilt and false guilt. True guilt is based solely on the facts. The fact is that none of us is perfect. In fact, no one is even close to perfect. Everyone has given plenty of poor performances. This is what constitutes true guilt. In *Happiness Is a Choice*, Frank B. Minirth and Paul D. Meier explain the nature of this emotion. True guilt involves a personal recognition of and remorse for the sin in one's life. It also involves a commitment to become sober, sensible, and self-controlled. The function of true guilt is not to make a person feel badly about himself. Its purpose is to point out areas for personal improvement.

False guilt, on the other hand, comes when people become overly self-critical. The person has turned against himself. False guilt is motivated by the need to constantly live according to rules and to impress others with "good" performances. Nowhere in the Bible is there any encouragement for people to accept false guilt. God did not give humans performance standards to try to make anyone feel wretched. Yet this is exactly what we do with one another.

All people have hidden sins that they hope will never be exposed. Also, everyone has fallen short of the perfect goals for right living. We can all identify with the apostle Paul, who wrote, "For that which I am doing, I do not understand; for I am not practicing what I would like to do, but I am doing the very thing I hate" (Rom. 7:15). Paul was describing the struggle between right and wrong that raged inside him. He knew he did not perform up to his own standards, much less the standards of God. It was painful for him to admit to himself that he didn't measure up!

Paul could have accepted the feeling of guilt, declaring himself to be a loser. But he didn't. He took comfort in the fact that God's love for him did not change. Instead, God worked even harder to demonstrate His love to Paul so that he wouldn't give up in despair. This is why Paul could conclude, "There is therefore now no condemnation for those who are in Christ Jesus" (Rom. 8:1).

Today too many people are so concerned about the judgment of other people that they lose sight of this promise from God. There is no reason for a person who is in Christ to accept the guilt given by misguided humans. If God says we are not condemned, because of the sacrifice of Jesus Christ, then why not believe it? Like most things, though, this is easier said than done.

Amy grew up in a broken home. Her parents divorced when she was eight, and she lived with her mother. She did not have many pleasant experiences in her mother's home. It seemed that she could never do anything to please her mom. Naturally Amy felt guilty each time her mother scolded her. She tried to upgrade her performances to make her mother like her, but nothing ever seemed to work. Her efforts were never enough. She was left with an emotional void.

Because Amy chronically felt guilty at home, she was not very assertive in making friends. She lived in fear that her friends would reject her as her mother did. So she became a follower. She thought that if she would do the things her friends wanted her to do, they would like her. This caused her to compromise her morals, which in turn caused her guilt feelings to increase. She continued to feel an emotional emptiness.

This emptiness caused Amy to feel desperate in her need to find a husband. She wanted someone who would be kind and loving, because she thought this would relieve her of her guilt. In college, she met and married a nice young man who was clearly on his way to success in his career. She saw that he had a sweet mother, so she assumed that if she could act just like her husband's mother, she could begin to feel good about herself.

Amy's efforts at performing for her husband's approval worked for a while. But by the time she reached her early thirties, she was worn out. She had worked so hard all her life at pleasing others that her lifestyle was tedious. She was physically and emotionally drained. And to make matters worse, she still felt badly about herself. Guilt had been a part of her life for so long that it finally seemed to be claiming a victory.

Amy went into a pattern of withdrawal. She drew away from her husband and became distant in communicating. She broke off ties with her church and friends. She even began neglecting her children because she resented having to do all the "nice things" a mother is supposed to do. Her whole personality seemed to change. Rather than always wearing a pleasing smile, she would anger quickly and become sarcastic. She had frequent temper flare-ups. She kept to herself a lot and wanted to have as little contact with people as possible.

What happened with Amy is common with many people. False guilt got the best of her. Early in her life she began believing and feeling that she was a bad person. With such a label, she was handicapped in her relationships. She felt the strong need to please others in order to prove she was not so bad. But once false guilt settles in, it is impossible to shake it by being a good actor.

All people know what it is like to put on a plastic smile when they really don't want to. People commonly worry about how they are going to look in the eyes of others. They are obsessed with looking good and saying the right things. Dishonesty can be a way of life. (Have you ever picked up the telephone and said a pleasant hello when you were really in a grouchy mood?)

Considering the extreme social pressure to be the right kind of person, it is easy to understand how some people come to have angry reactions. The anger is usually their way of telling the world that they are tired of being phony. The problem arises when this anger is expressed too often and too destructively. Think of the peace of mind that could come by stepping off of the treadmill.

9

The Near-sighted
Syndrome

$\mathbb{D}$r. Edwin Young, a pastor in Houston, Texas, once said that one of the greatest enemies to marriage relationships is the thermostat. Many petty differences in preference of air temperature have caused normally calm partners to blow up at one another in fits of rage. Each partner is so insistent about having his own way that he makes a mountain out of a molehill. Each may have a valid point that he wishes to discuss, but both lose all sense of reason when they feel that they are not being listened to. They have a driving compulsion to *make* the other person agree. Sound familiar?

It is utterly amazing to think of the number of relationships that have been damaged beyond repair due to persistent squabbles over something as minor as the thermostat. Some people will argue for hours and not realize the destructiveness of it all. And it is not just married couples who get bogged down in this type of feuding. Parents will argue endlessly with their children over small issues. Brothers and sisters are famous for fighting over such huge matters as who gets to sit in the front seat of the car. Many an office has been disrupted by individuals whose feelings are hurt because of a minor mistake made, or because they did not get their way in some decision.

It is amazing to note how highly skilled people can be at taking small matters and blowing them up into big ones. We are constantly being bombarded with television news about groups that are protesting about their rights being violated. Books have flooded the market to teach consumers to get what they want. We are part of a generation that is determined to stand up and fight. As a whole, the human race seems to find it difficult to control the impulse to angrily confront every little aggravation that arises.

This need to fight first and think later can be called the near-sighted syndrome. It is the compulsion that comes over people when they lose perspective on their priorities in life. I already have mentioned that anger is not necessarily a wrong emotion. It is an emotional response that people have when they feel they have been wronged. It represents the emotional need to stand up for ourselves and voice our convictions. But, as with most good things, it can be overused.

Our minor problems can be like a small stone. If we hold the stone directly in front of our eyes, it blocks our vision. If the stone is held at arm's length, it can be examined for what it really is. If the stone is thrown onto the ground, in its true setting, it can be seen as a small bump underfoot.

It is easy to determine a person's priorities by watching the things that cause him anger. People who are angry about matters such as being three minutes late for an appointment or having the house look a little unkempt are showing their true colors. Through their anger they are letting the world know that getting their way is their number-one priority. By contrasting this attitude with the anger of Jesus Christ, we can see a better set of priorities. The things that caused Jesus the most anger were self-righteousness (smugness) and blasphemy. This showed that His priorities centered around the love and redemption found in a relationship with God.

The vast majority of people in the world today are living without any well-defined personal goals. Some may have the goal of owning a nice house and making a lot of money. Others may have the goal of being popular and friendly. But beyond that, what is there? Surely there must be something more to live for than money and favor with people.

The question that has plagued philosophers for centuries is: "What is life?" From day one humans have had the need to find meaning and purpose in life. If we were to closely examine the behaviors of most people we would find that they thrive on looking out for themselves. After all, that is what is at the core of the sin nature. Because each person has his own selfish commitment to get what he wants, even if it means other people are pushed aside, he is also capable of lots of anger. Anger is inevitable when there are billions of people looking out for themselves.

In order to put life in its proper perspective we need to understand what God has in mind for us. Jesus said, "I came that they might have life, and might have it abundantly" (John 10:10).

From the beginning of time God had one purpose for all people. We were created in order to have the privilege of having a relationship with God and knowing His love. I was talking about this concept once with a woman who stated that it seemed conceited that God would create us so that we could have the privilege of knowing Him. Indeed, if God had sinful qualities this would be laughable. But the fact is that God is perfect. He is love. Therefore, we can see His creation of the world as a loving gift He gives to mankind.

Those people who have chronic problems with destructive anger do not have a good grasp of this love that God has for them. When anyone becomes consumed with knowing and experiencing the love of God, the small irritants of his life will be much more tolerable. For you see, the more people experience God's love, the more motivated they will be to pass it on to those around them. This is what God had in mind for us. This is why He created human relationships. By being loving to and understanding with one another, we can help each other to know in a tangible way the love of God.

How quickly we get our priorities out of line! Many people have an intellectual knowledge of the love of God, but it is something they use only on Sunday mornings. The rest of the week they are concerned with meeting their selfish desires. They are afraid that if they do live a life that shows the love of God, they will be in such a minority that their lives will become "all give and no get." They are mistrustful of this lifestyle and they are afraid it might backfire.

Let's assume that anger influenced by this near-sighted syndrome is the opposite of love. (Actually it is the main problem that keeps us from experiencing love.) If we go to the love chapter in the Bible, I Corinthians 13 (specifically verses 4–6), and *reverse* its definition of love, we can easily spell out the traits found in people who suffer from this condition. We would find that the near-sighted syndrome

is impatient, never seeking to understand.

is not kind, but mean and inconsiderate.

is jealous and possessive.

is boastful and puffed up.

acts in an ugly way and seeks only after self.

is easily provoked, short-tempered.

holds grudges and keeps detailed records of another's
wrongs.

is unconcerned when someone suffers an injustice.
(They probably deserve it anyway.)

People with the near-sighted syndrome have a need to
look at life from the big picture. In the big picture, they
will find that all people are imperfect. All have a need for
God's love and forgiveness. Consequently, no one person is
any better than another. We are all the same. By viewing
the big picture of life, most people will come to humble
themselves. They will realize that they have no business
making life harder than it already is for others. They will
recognize that in order to tackle the problems life has to
offer, we need teamwork. This can cause the individual to
work hard on recognizing his responsibilities. The person
who looks at the big picture of life will acknowledge five
points.

1. When problems arise, a calm head usually prevails.
2. The more a person frets about a problem, the worse
   it gets. Fretting is like scratching an insect bite.
3. If someone does something he does not like, it was
   not necessarily meant as an insult.
4. Even if another person does insult him, no one can
   make him feel controlled by a negative feeling.
5. There is always hope unless one chooses to give up.

Too many people are living their lives without a well
thought-out game plan. They haphazardly go along in life
making off-the-cuff reactions to problems that arise.
Without any goal there is a good chance that they will
meet with a great deal of frustration. There are absolutely

no guarantees. But through Christianity, we can devise an excellent game plan. We are told, "Be ye therefore perfect, even as your Father which is in heaven is perfect" (Matt. 5:48, KJV). The word *perfect* in this verse is better translated as "mature." We are told to put ourselves into a maturing process, trying to live the love that is God. This is our goal.

PART Three

How People Handle Anger
(Or How Anger Handles People)

10

Repress It, Express It, Or Release It

It can be well and good to understand why anger exists. But we are still left with the questions: What's a person to do when anger comes on? Is it proper to let it all out and get it out of one's system, as some experts suggest? Should a person close himself into the nearest closet and scream at the top of his lungs? Or should a person try to keep anger from being expressed at all, and try to show extra love and patience instead? The answer to these questions is: "It all depends."

There is no one correct way to handle anger. Obviously the circumstances are going to have an influence on how one chooses to deal with anger. For example, a crowded elevator is not exactly the best place to let it all out when you are angry with your spouse. Nor is it usually wise to explode with pent-up hostility toward a boss who is hurrying down the hall to a meeting (particularly if it's a job you want to keep). In some cases it might be proper to simply drop the anger and move on to something else, while at other times it may be appropriate to speak boldly and firmly.

There are three general styles in which people can handle anger: repression, expression, and release. Each can be dangerous in its own way. So we need to look closely at each of these three to determine how it fits (or does not fit) into a pattern of proper anger.

Repressed Anger

Many people are afraid of anger and try to avoid it at all costs. When the emotion surfaces they do their best to pretend it is not there. Their reasoning (conscious or subconscious) is that if one ignores anger it will go away. To these people, anger is an ugly wolf. It is something terribly destructive. Most of these people either have been taught openly to avoid anger or have learned through bitter experience how painful anger can be. I know one woman who had been the youngest of six children. She sensed that her mother had not wanted her and resented her. In order to keep her mother happy, this woman always tried to be extra nice and sweet. She never allowed herself to be angry or sad because she was afraid of displeasing her mother. As an adult she kept up the same pattern until she broke down in deep depression. She had repressed her anger so much that it caused her to live a life of a phony. This became more than she could bear.

Repression is a form of denial. If a person denies that he is angry, then he feels no obligation to deal with his anger. The problem is solved (temporarily). Naturally this is a dangerous method of handling anger. Repression may have its short-term rewards, but in the long run repressed anger is usually especially powerful and bitter. By repressing it, a person is pushing anger from the conscious to the subconscious. There it can fester and worsen without that person's knowledge.

Once anger is pushed into the unconscious mind, the emotion is out of that person's immediate control. In fact, when it is "out of sight" a person may become convinced that he is free from anger. Not so! Whenever you hear a person state that he never gets angry you can be assured that he is repressing his anger. Religious people are especially prone to this since they assume anger is unchristian. How wrong this can be! These are the people who have chronic trouble with ulcers or headaches. These are the people who are prone to sit piously in judgment over others. These are the people who may surprise everyone when they suddenly have an angry outburst that seemingly comes from nowhere! The truth is that repression and Christianity don't mix well.

One example is Neal. He was in his midforties and had three teen-age children. He came to my office one day seeking counseling because his family did not get along. The teen-agers were constantly arguing, dragging Neal and his wife into one battle after another. Neal did not seek counseling to deal with his emotions (which were a mixed-up wreck). Rather, his stated goal was to learn how to exhibit more patience so he could be a better household leader. He actually claimed that he was very stable emotionally and he prided himself on his ability to be involved in a conflict without getting angry.

You can guess that Neal was not handling his anger well at all. He was simply pretending it didn't exist whenever it would arise. Here was a man who thought he was handling himself in as Christian a way as possible. He equated Christian love with patience (translated: never angry). Never would he raise his voice or inflict any type of serious punishment. In his thinking, that might indicate a lack of love. To him anger was something awful.

As Neal and I talked, he admitted with much guilt that he wished he could leave his family. He hated to say it, but sometimes they made him so angry that he couldn't stand the sight of them. As he let his true feelings come out, tears flowed. He was ashamed that he could be capable of such feelings. As a youngster Neal had witnessed some poor examples of adults blowing up in anger and he had vowed he would never act that way. In truth, there were many times when he wanted to show anger, but he was afraid of being rejected if he did. With good intentions he did his best to show love by being the quiet, calm daddy. His strategy had really backfired.

After he had opened himself up to me this way, I responded to Neal with something that stunned him. I congratulated him for telling me about his anger. And I thanked him for sharing it with me. After overcoming his surprise, he started going through his old routine about how it was wrong for him to ever feel that way. I reassured him that while we sometimes contemplate wrong behavior when we are angry, the anger itself is not necessarily wrong. In fact, I went on to tell him that he would be a more responsible father and husband if he would express his anger from time to time. Again he resisted, reminding me of how he had vowed to never let his wife and children see him angry. Needless to say, Neal did not learn to give himself permission to become angry after one session. But in time, he came to understand that, by trying to pretend he was never angry, he was sitting on top of a powder keg that was waiting to explode. He learned that by repressing anger he did not rid himself of it.

Repressed anger is virtually never desirable. No emotion can be dealt with properly by simply "forgetting" it. Forgetting and repression are not one and the same. If one truly forgets something it is out of the mind. If one represses something it is out of the conscious mind, but it still remains active in the subconscious mind.

Expressed Anger

We are living in a day and age when it is increasingly popular to get feelings out in the open. "Express yourself" was the cry of the late sixties and the seventies. Volumes have been written about saying whatever is on your mind and about getting what you have coming to you. We have witnessed one special-interest group after another angrily and unashamedly demanding its rights. As a culture, Americans are quickly losing any sense of bashfulness. The prevailing mood is that if you have been offended, get angry! Certainly we are in a period where it is acceptable, even fashionable, to "let it all hang out."

This expressive mood could be fine if people knew what they were doing. Unfortunately that is not always the case. Earlier in the book, I pointed out that anger can be assertive or it can be aggressive. Assertive anger means that people stand up firmly for their convictions in a manner that respects another's dignity. Aggressive anger may also be stated firmly, but without true regard for the other person's worth. Therefore, when people express anger, that expression may be correct or incorrect, depending on the level of sensitivity to others. Nonetheless, expressed anger is anger that is communicated outwardly.

Anger is not always expressed verbally. It can be expressed through behavior. Well over half of all communication is done through nonverbal means. Nonverbal expressions of anger can include a stern look, a slam of a door, ignoring someone, crying, or giving a cold glare. There are an infinite number of ways to express anger. Imagination is the only limit to the number of ways this emotion can be communicated.

Because people are so capable of expressing anger in a destructive way, certain guidelines should be followed to make sure anger works for us instead of against us.

1. Be sure that when you express anger you do not attempt to establish your own superiority. This could cause the recipient of your anger to harbor resentment. The more resentment the recipient feels, the more he will become wrapped up in his own defenses. This means that you won't be listened to or understood. It can create a battle of one-upmanship.

2. Make sure that your anger has a constructive aim. Anger expressed for the sake of meanness is just going to create an atmosphere that will breed more anger. Remember, anger is a God-given emotion that is to be used as a building tool, not a wrecking ball.

3. Be aware of the responsiveness of the recipient. That is, make sure the other party is ready to hear what you have to say. Sometimes you will find people who are never ready to listen to you. At that point you will need to decide whether it is best to go ahead and express yourself or to drop the subject. For example, Jesus sometimes had angry things to say to the Pharisees. No doubt there were plenty of times when He could have said something but decided to save His breath.

4. Consider the feelings and circumstances of the recipient. There will be times when your anger may be completely correct, but you will not be able to communicate it constructively due to the mindset of the other person. Most wives have learned that it is better to unload the frustrations of their day onto their husbands after the husbands have had a little while to sit down and unwind from a long day's work.

Knowing when and how to express anger is the key. And just because it is sometimes correct to let it out doesn't mean that it is always correct. Sensitivity is the main trait that an angry person needs to hold onto.

Released Anger

Released anger refers to anger that is dismissed, or let go. It is not to be confused with repressed anger. Repressed anger is simply pushed into the subconscious mind. But when anger is released, the person has made the conscious decision that anger is no longer needed and it is therefore dropped. People can gain the ability to release anger only after they first gain some mastery of the art of expressing anger. After anger has served its purpose (or if one sees that it has no good purpose) the mature individual will have enough sense to let go of it.

Very little has been written about dismissing anger. It doesn't get the publicity that goes to the topic of expressing anger. But there always will be instances when the best way to handle anger is to release it. For example, there are some people who will never change their ways. When this is the case it is best not to waste emotional energy on them. We all can probably think of someone who never has cared for anyone's feelings and probably never will.

The idea of being able to let go of anger confuses some people. They question their ability to turn off their feelings like a faucet. They may conclude that it is impossible to decide to not have a particular feeling. To be sure, we are not able to invite our feelings to come and go as we see fit. Feelings, particularly anger, are too unpredictable for that. But we can control our feelings. If we believe we can't control our feelings we might as well give up trying to improve our lives.

All sane human beings are capable of getting their feelings under control. If anger is too strong it is possible for a person to calm down by using willpower. One of the characteristics that God has given humans is the ability to make choices. This includes the ability to make choices regarding anger. People who say they *can't* control their anger actually *won't* control it. By allowing anger to reign supreme they are choosing to be untamed and rebellious. The people who remain constant slaves to anger are those who refuse to accept the responsibility for deciding their own destiny.

Sometimes it feels unnatural to control anger. Our tendency is to hold on to anger for prolonged periods of time. If someone has wronged us, we want him to suffer. Hanging on to anger is a good way to make someone squirm and feel as if he is on the hot seat. But if we remember the cautions the Bible uses in instructing us on anger, we will admit there are too many times when anger causes more harm than good.

For instance, Cathy had been dating Lee for several years. (Both had been divorced.) Cathy had sensed for a long time that Lee was losing interest in her and was becoming more interested in Nancy. This angered Cathy as she thought of all the effort she had put into her relationship with him. One evening Lee and Nancy were eating dinner in a small cafe when Cathy happened to see them. She instantly was filled with rage, rushed to the table, and began choking Nancy. She later told me that if she had had a gun she would have killed them both.

Cathy could have listed several reasons why she had the "right" to be angry with her boyfriend. She felt rejected and betrayed. But her problem was that she forgot her responsibilities to Lee, to Nancy, and to herself. She had allowed her anger to swell so strongly inside herself that it became extremely inappropriate. Previously she had tried to express her anger to Lee, but he was determined to ignore her feelings. In hindsight it is clear that Cathy would have been better off to release some of her anger. Apparently the strength of her anger was harming her chances to rebuild her relationship with Lee. It only drove him away. It was no longer useful.

One of the things that makes it difficult to release anger is people's reluctance to face reality. They think (as Cathy did), "Maybe if I *really* show some anger I can get what I want." The reality is that some people are going to do what they want regardless of anyone else's emotions. It seems mechanical to decide to let go of these emotions. It may not be what we want, yet it may be necessary for our emotional stability.

Understanding the three general ways of handling anger makes it possible for you to examine your patterns of dealing with anger. Certainly it is not always best to express anger. There are times when that would do more harm than good. It definitely is not best to try to repress anger so that it is merely out of the conscious mind. And there are times when it is right and times when it is wrong to release it. We each need to come up with our own personalized game plan for how we will handle anger. The better control we have over it, the more anger will work in our favor.

11

Hit and Run

Shouting? Do you think I'm shouting? Wait 'til you hear me when I *really* get mad!" These are the words of a man with a volcanic temper as he erupts at his scared wife after she asks him not to shout when he gets angry. This is a scene that is played out all too frequently in homes across the country. Anger and violent outbursts are dangerous companions.

People who express anger in biting, abrasive ways are very insecure. They feel fragile, vulnerable, and unloved. But they cover up their feelings by attempting to dominate or degrade others. It is an obvious attempt to hide feelings of inferiority by trying to appear superior. It is impossible to have positive interchanges between two people when one or both of them are expressing their anger this way. People who use this approach to anger have a "hit-and-run" philosophy. They hit with anger and run from intimacy.

When biting anger is expressed, it is a good guess that the person using it is afraid of intimacy. Most people know when their expression of anger is appropriate or not. And when they go ahead and communicate inappropriately anyway, they are exhibiting an "I-don't-care" attitude. They have given up the hope for emotional closeness and have pulled out all stops. To stop expressing anger in this

103

way, these people will need to commit themselves to fostering intimacy.

The styles of anger explored in this chapter fall into the category of active-aggressive anger. True to aggressive style, there is little regard for the impact the anger will have on other people. The sad thing is that the anger itself may be correct. The angry person may have some legitimate grievances. But the expression is so wrong that the correct message is never communicated.

Verbal Outbursts

People who make verbal outbursts are easy to spot. They are the ones who get red in the face, raise their voices to a booming pitch, and say all kinds of nasty, insulting things when they are angry. People who use this technique are highly frustrated (to make an understatement). They have strong feelings, yet they feel as though they are not being taken seriously. Most of these people have tried to express their anger calmly, but for some reason or another, it didn't work. As a last resort they verbally blast their victims in order to inflict some pain. Their unconscious goal is to make the other person feel so badly that he cannot help but respond in the "correct" way.

Some of these people have legitimate complaints that cause them to feel like blasting away. Most will say that they feel misunderstood. They will say that the reason they resort to such outbursts is to get the undivided attention of the person who has made them feel rejected. At the same time, however, many of these people are slow to admit that when they express anger, they have one and only one response they wish to hear. The reason that they make violent outbursts is that they did not get their specified response. They are asking for total submission rather than honest communication.

The ultimate form of blasting is physical violence. Acts of physical violence virtually always begin with verbal cheap shots. Once people allow their anger to grow to this point, it is hard to control the urge to physically "put someone in his place." This only accomplishes the opposite of healthy relationships. It builds thick, high walls.

Blame

Some people are hopelessly irresponsible. If anything goes wrong, they insist that someone else will have to be held accountable. These are the people who are experts at blame. Whenever a problem arises they manage to point the accusing finger. In truth, they are afraid that their own weaknesses might be exposed. They know they have so many flaws already that they cannot bear the idea that they could be held responsible for more. As long as they can keep the focus away from themselves, they will be under no pressure to be responsible. It is a convenient technique for anyone who has something to hide.

People who use blame like to think in terms of who's at fault. If a problem occurs, obviously someone else messed up. If a weakness is shown, there must be an inexcusable reason for it. They think it is impossible for a problem to occur without someone being a bad guy. Accidents don't just happen. They are caused by wily demons.

Sarcasm

Sarcasm is for people who are angry but are afraid to be open and honest about it. Rather than owning up to the feeling, it seems easier to make a cutting remark or a blistering comment. Some sarcastic people fancy themselves as traveling stand-up comedians. Through the use of scathing jokes and one-liners they are able to let their feelings seep out, while getting some revenge.

When a person frequently uses sarcasm, you can bet that there is a lot of bitterness just beneath the surface. One man told me that he began using sarcasm as a teen-ager because it seemed to be his only release for feelings of bitterness toward parents and teachers who were too controlling. He didn't feel free to express himself properly. But as time went on, he continued with his sarcasm, even though it was not necessary. He had continued to harbor bitter feelings toward people in authority and, because he was afraid to be honest with his feelings, sarcasm was the only weapon he had.

Sarcasm also indicates a feeling of disillusionment. That is, these people may at one time have had high hopes and expectations for someone, only to be let down. Along with the obvious anger, there is a sense of loneliness due to missed opportunities. By striking back in sarcasm, people are trying to avoid dealing with their hurt and disappointment.

Poisonous Talk

Anger is often diluted into poisonous talk. There are some people who seem to do nothing but talk, talk, talk. And the things they say can be harsh! Sometimes the hostility is easy to spot: "You will never amount to any-thing." But at other times it is quite subtle: "This is a delicious casserole, but doesn't it need a little more paprika?"

People who use this style of anger use honesty as a cover for anger. If someone would dare to rebuke them for what they say, they can always retort, "Well, what do you want me to do, tell lies?" But even though the words they speak are true, they are still being dishonest. Honesty involves more than just speaking truthful words. It in-volves being honest with feelings, too. People who are the objects of poisonous talk very often are not able to engage in meaningful conversation because they are disarmed from the beginning. If they angrily confront the person, the poisonous talker will deny any malicious intent. If they accept the poisonous talk at face value, they are playing into the game. The relationship is killed.

Gossip

Very closely related to poisonous talk is gossip. Gossip is a means of putting someone down by spreading idle rumors. More reputations have been spoiled by the spreading of false stories than by any other act. The poor person who is being gossiped about is given no chance to stand up for himself. Consequently, people hear only half-truths. And to be honest, most people who gossip don't really want to know the truth. It's usually not as juicy.

Gossipers often deny their angry intentions by first saying, "I don't mean to spread rumors, but I think you should know that. . . ." They claim innocence. On the surface everything seems harmless. But indeed, most gossipers realize that they are harming others. Secretly, that is their intent! If these people truly had good intentions they first would have put a stop to the rumor mill and have clarified things with the object of the gossip.

Complaints

One of the most obnoxious ways to express anger is to whine and complain. There are some people who can find something to grumble about in any situation. Some of these people probably won't be satisfied with heaven! The chronic complainer has much hidden hostility. More than likely these people have been very dissatisfied with the way life has gone for them. They feel cheated and hurt, so there is no motivation to ever look on the bright side. They know from bitter experience that the bright side of life includes only false hopes.

Complainers say they would like to look on the bright side of life if they could be convinced that it exists. But even when things seem to take a turn for the better, they still hold on to the spirit of pessimism. It is like the attitude of the man who came home from the office with a snarl on his face. When his wife asked him about his problem he told her he got a raise in salary—but it just served to remind him that he didn't make as much money as his brother. People like him like to relieve their angry feelings by dumping them on innocent bystanders.

Stubbornness

Some people won't admit they are wrong even if it is obvious. They would be taking the risk of opening themselves to meaningful communication. And to some people, that's scary! One woman told me that she knew she was treating her husband wrongly. She knew that she tended to be judgmental and harsh in the way she spoke to him. But she claimed she had no other choice other than to stubbornly argue with him for fear that she would appear weak. The truth is, she enjoyed holding on to the power that her anger provided.

Notice how power struggles are at the heart of many broken relationships. Anger, in its pure form, consists of firmly standing up for one's convictions. But in its warped form it is used as a tool for providing pseudostrength. Some people have the misconception that their friends and relatives were made for stroking their egos. They will do nothing to lower themselves into a humble, serving position because that would work against their hunger for power.

Intimidation

Most people are familiar with the stereotyped image of the supervisor who fusses and grumbles about everything. He seems to think that the only way to make people work well is to scare them half to death. The last thing these intimidators would do would be to admit that they have normal emotions. They are fearful that if anyone found out that beneath the booming, fear-invoking voice is a regular person, they might be rejected. Of course, everyone knows that these kinds of people are found not only at work, but also at home, in the church, or anywhere else.

The philosophy behind this kind of behavior is: "Overwhelm other people before they have a chance to challenge you." These people feel a strong need to be recognized as someone important. Yet at the same time they feel the need to keep people at a distance. Because they have a great deal of unresolved hostility, they assume other people are hostile, too. So their strategy is to create an atmosphere such that people are afraid to express their feelings. Temporarily it provides them with a safe shelter. In the long run, however, they become very lonely and disillusioned.

Criticism

The anger in the constant critic is usually obvious. Critics are provoked about things that do not happen according to plan, so their solution is to call attention to the negative. Yet people who criticize continually are usually reluctant to admit their anger. They say, "It's not that I'm angry. I just call 'em the way I see 'em."

Being critical is easy to do. There are indeed so many things wrong with people and things that people can find problems without even looking for them. The difference between constant critics and everyone else is that critics have not developed adequate ways of accepting life's imperfections. Consequently, they feel defeated in their lives. Subconsciously they live by the rule: "Misery loves company." If they feel incapable of climbing out of the dungeon of pessimism, the next best thing is to pull the world down to their level.

One problem keeps many critics from being helped. That is, they usually refuse to admit that their criticism stems from a feeling of inadequacy. They assume a superior position. But we all know that since there is no person who in God's eyes is superior to another, we can rest assured that any feeling of superiority is false. Their behavior is only a desperate attempt to keep the focus off of their own dreaded weaknesses.

Rumination

Rumination occurs when people talk on and on about the past without any apparent awareness that they are boring others to tears. Many people instantly think of older people when they think of people who ruminate. But that's not fair. Like all other styles of anger, ruminating is done by people of all shapes, sizes, and ages.

On the surface, going on and on about the past seems harmless. After all, it could be interpreted as an attempt by some lonely soul to get someone to listen. But most people who resort to ruminating feel unsure that anyone will pay attention to them. More than likely they have had experiences when others have rudely or carelessly shut them out. By talking and talking, these people are making absolutely certain that they won't be shut out again.

Have you ever tried to leave the room when someone was in the middle of his ruminating? It's almost impossible! This person knows (perhaps only subconsciously) that he is talking too much. But he exercises no control over his mouth. Regardless of the feelings of those around, he is determined to continue. He is so intent on saying what he wants to say that he has become oblivious to his sense of responsibility to others. He simply doesn't care anymore!

There is a major drawback (aside from the obvious) with each of these "hit-and-run" types of anger. Even though the anger is expressed, it is not released. The anger is never dealt with properly. Like other emotions, anger cannot be worked through indirectly. It needs to be tackled head-on. One reason God made humans capable of intimacy was to give us chances to work through the feelings we experience. Feelings are a means to an end. They are intended to be tools for self-examination and for building relationships. As long as people handle emotions in sinister ways, problems will be perpetuated rather than solved.

12

Silent But Deadly

$\mathbb{A}$nger is not always boisterous. There is no rule that states a person has to raise his voice and pound his fist on the table in order to express anger. Anger can take on some very subtle forms of expression. Quite often it is expressed in a quiet, passive way. Silent anger can be very effective if one's goal is to "even the score" with someone else. It can leave the opponent feeling totally helpless, unable to break through the barrier erected. When you examine it closely, you can find that silent anger is actually the most controlling form of anger there is!

Silent anger is characterized by passive-aggressive behavior. On the surface, the person with this pattern appears normal. But usually this person has a hard time openly expressing feelings. Usually passive-aggressive people are attracted to others who have strong leadership qualities, because they tend to resist doing things on their own initiative. For the most part, they are very dependent on others for their sense of emotional stability. Yet at the same time they resist being controlled. They want others to do the work in making relationships work. That way, if something goes wrong it can be blamed on the other person. It is a perfect style of living for someone who wants to avoid responsibility in the difficulties of life.

Passive-aggressive persons are afraid to be honest about

their emotions. They know that if they share their feelings, risks will be involved. They might be rejected or taken advantage of. For example, if these people express displeasure with what a friend is doing, they are afraid the friendship will automatically fall apart. These people have a hard time seeing anger as a responsibility. As far as they are concerned, there is nothing good about direct conflict. It is to be avoided at all costs.

These people express their anger, but in an emotionally lazy way. Rather than confronting others, they opt for a safer way out. The problem with these "safe" approaches to anger is that they create more trouble than they solve.

Some people actually take pride in the fact that they do not outwardly express anger. They see this as a sign of strength. Yet when anger exists in a person (it is in each of us) and is not expressed properly, it is still going to come out. More than likely, the passive anger will be just as deadly, or more so, than open and direct anger potentially could be. Following are some of the many passive-aggressive expressions of anger.

The Silent Treatment

The classic expression of passive anger is the silent treatment. I could not even begin to count the number of married couples that I have spoken with in which at least one of the partners used the silent treatment as a regular means of expressing anger. It is perhaps the most effective weapon that an individual can use to exert emotional control over someone else. Many spouses have complained that they have wanted to talk out a problem situation with their mate, only to be met by a "deaf" ear. In addition, many employees have been left shaking in their boots by a boss who refused to speak to them when something had gone wrong. Many a friendship has come to an end when one or both parties became angry and decided they would not speak until they had gotten their way.

Keep in mind that a person does not have to be speaking in order to communicate to someone else. In fact, there is no such thing as "no communication." We are constantly in communication with one another simply by the way we present ourselves. A person who remains stubbornly silent when it is clear that a verbal exchange is needed is communicating a great deal of anger. Silence is a way of stating that the other person (the object of the anger) is not worthy enough to talk to. The silence is also communicating strong disapproval to the other person. The person on the receiving end of the silent treatment has no way to fight back. He is totally disarmed. This of course causes further irritation, and the conflict may intensify.

Notice the facial expressions that people have when they are using this style of behavior. The eyebrows are usually turned in. The forehead is wrinkled. The people who use this form of anger are creating more trouble than they realize. They may excuse this behavior by saying that they wish to have no part of a circular argument. But actually they are creating a situation that resembles the legendary feud between the McCoys and the Hatfields. They had forgotten why they were angry with each other, but they knew that they used to have some good reason. In addition, though, these people are harming themselves. By remaining silent, they are allowing bitterness to fester inside. Their faces say that something is wrong, but their silence says that they are not going to do anything constructive about it. In the end, all involved are losers.

Procrastination

All of us have known people who have a tendency to put off until tomorrow what they don't want to do today. (Certainly, though, you have never been guilty of this.) We might even go so far to say that some people's aim in life is to pursue pleasure while it is here and to worry about responsibilities when there is nothing else to do. This kind of behavior is simply a lazy form of rebellion. Perhaps a husband resents being asked to help clean the house, so he comes up with other, "more important" things to occupy his time. Or maybe friends are angry with one another, so one decides to delay doing the favor that was requested.

Procrastination easily fits into the passive-aggressive pattern, since it is possible to procrastinate without saying a word or lifting a finger. It, too, can be very controlling, particularly if the task delayed is something another person is depending on. Like other forms of inappropriate anger, procrastination can be an effective way of gaining the upper hand in a conflict. Often procrastinators defend themselves by protesting that they genuinely intend to do the right things, but they just don't have the time. Sometimes that may be the case, but the truth of the matter is that we tend to do the things that we give priority to. By putting a task off, a procrastinator can be telling others that they are not very high on the list of priorities!

Halfhearted Efforts

I can recall that one of my responsibilities as a child was to dry the dishes after mealtime. It usually made me angry that I had to do this because I felt that I had much more important things to do outdoors with my friends. More often than not I would express my anger by doing the absolute minimum that would get me out of the kitchen. Being angry, I had a "don't-care" attitude about my job.

This sort of attitude is widespread. Many workers who are frustrated with working conditions would rather be hung by their thumbs than give a solid day of effort on the job. Doing a half-job is their way of getting even. Children may resent responsibilities handed to them at home or at school, so they will figure the easy way out and pursue that. Spouses may decide that their partner has quit making honest efforts toward having a good marriage, so they decide that they will quit trying, too.

These kinds of behaviors are practiced by individuals who either are afraid to let their feelings out or believe that it won't do any good to express themselves. It is a quitter's approach to life. In some form or fashion they feel cheated, and inefficiency is their way of standing up to the world ("I'll show you!"). There is always the risk that if they let their feelings out in the open, they will be discounted, or worse, they will be proven wrong. Their pattern of inefficiency can give them a perfect chance to demonstrate their "effort" while indirectly ventilating their anger.

Depression

Many people are surprised to learn that depression is simply a form of anger. This can be illustrated by one woman who came to our clinic after going through two years of chronic depression. In her childhood, she had much inconsistency from her parents. She felt that they did not want her because one of her sisters always seemed to be the favored one. Naturally this angered her, but she felt inept at expressing her anger to her parents. So she repressed her anger. Later, in college, she married, hoping that her husband would cure her problems. But he had his inadequacies, so again she felt cheated. She thought that perhaps having children would make her feel useful, but after they began growing up she knew they could get along without her. Once again anger surfaced. She tried religion, she got involved in community affairs, but everywhere she turned she felt insignificant or replaceable.

After years of struggling with one frustration after another she collapsed into depression. It was her ultimate expression of anger.

Depression is a passive way of communicating that one has found the world (or at least parts of it) to be no good. It is an act of aggression in that a depressed person is withdrawing from others, thereby not allowing anyone to enjoy the benefits of having his friendship. It is a backward way of showing disdain for the conditions he has to "put up with" in his life. It is a style of selfishness because the depressed person is not allowing others to learn what they can do to help build the relationship. It is temporarily more convenient to repress rather than express the anger and to live in a protective shell, isolated as it may be.

There actually can be some "advantages" to being depressed. Depressed people don't have to concern themselves with anyone else. This allows them plenty of time to stew in self-pity. It also is a good excuse to get out of taking on unwanted responsibilities. After all, when people see that someone is depressed they will lower their expectations for him or look for someone else to take up a certain task. In all fairness, sometimes depression can be legitimate, but usually it is a passive cop-out for a person who does not want to deal head-on with risky feelings.

Compliance

Many people who are compliant can be pleasant to be with. But watch out! A person who constantly agrees with others may be a volcano waiting to explode. In true passive-aggressive style, these people are afraid to be honest with others about their feelings. They know that they are running the risk of being emotionally vulnerable if they do. To them, anger is something to be dreaded and avoided at all costs. Therefore these people will often sell themselves to a pattern of living that is actually beneath their standards. A good illustration of this is the sexually active person, the drug or alcohol abuser, or someone as inconspicuous as the typical "nice guy." These people are characterized by the inability to say no when they are encouraged to do something that is against their principles.

On the surface, it would seem that people comply with others in order to avoid the anger that may come from others. But don't be fooled. Compliant persons may actually be going along with the crowd in order to avoid expressing their *own* anger. They are afraid that if they are direct with anger it could be abrasive or insulting. It could cost them friendships. At least this is what they tell themselves. By doing what they are told to do, compliant people may actually be behaving in a highly irresponsible way by depriving other people of honesty in the relationship. This is actually a form of communicating a lack of concern for other people, since it disregards their need to hear honest feelings.

For example, Sarah met a man who had a prison record. By the time she met him he was involved in more deviant activity. Knowing of his mannerisms, Sarah decided that she would live with this man and see what it was like to live on the wild side of life. So she willingly gave her life over to him. At this point, compliance was a form of rebellion against her family. After a while she began realizing how big a mistake she had made. Her boyfriend involved her in illicit sexual relations and in activities that involved illegal drugs. At first she went along with him for the adventure. After she tired of him, she continued to comply with him, but all the while she was hoping that her irresponsible behavior would draw attention to the deviant ways of her boyfriend. She secretly wished that by being bad herself, she could help get this man back in jail. She was afraid that if she did not go along with him, he might actually reform (heaven forbid!) and therefore he would not get what was coming to him.

Conformity that started out as a pleasure ride wound up being a well-planned scheme of aggression. Once a person becomes involved in secretive activity, it is hard to give it up. What seems to be compliant behavior may actually be a disguise for a deep fear of confrontation and honesty.

Forgetfulness

It is rare for someone to forget to do something for someone when he has a genuine desire to be kind and helpful. This does not mean that every time a person forgets that he is being aggressive. Naturally, some forgetfulness is normal. (Some psychologists insist, however, that there is no such thing as innocent forgetfulness.) Suffice it to say that a person who has a well-ingrained pattern of forgetfulness probably can be categorized as one with an anger problem.

Forgetfulness can be a convenient way to punish someone for not being the kind of person that he "ought" to be. One man was constantly forgetting to do little favors that his wife would ask him to do. When he finally got up enough courage to speak his mind, this man said that it didn't bother him that he was forgetful. He resented the way his wife nagged him, so he didn't want to do anything kind for her anyway. Rather than dealing openly with his resentment, he repressed it and let his anger sneak out in this way.

Notice what forgetfulness can communicate. Like other forms of passive-aggressive behavior, it can be a way of stating that other people's desires are not very high on one's list of priorities. Chronic forgetfulness is a sure-fire indicator of the "don't-care" attitude. Forgetful people often offer weak excuses about events or responsibilities simply slipping their minds. However, my guess is that if these same people were asked to remember to do something for the Queen of England there would be little doubt about whether it would be done. Remembering to do something is simply a matter of priorities. Forgetfulness is a way of asserting that one does not share the same priorities with other people.

Preoccupation

I was once in a meeting where I noticed one man, sitting in a chair off to the side, who kept his head facing down during the entire meeting. He would periodically doodle with his pen on a notepad, but it was quite obvious that his mind was miles away. Afterward, I jokingly remarked to this man that he really seemed to be interested in the issues discussed during this time. He gruffly responded that in his opinion all meetings were a waste of time and if he had to come to one, he didn't want to say anything for fear that it would just drag the time out. His anger was obvious.

We all have been in situations that we wished we could escape from. In fact, if we don't watch ourselves we can easily become angry for having to put up with circumstances that are not to our liking. A classic example of this kind of anger is the intelligent child who makes poor grades in school not because of his inability but because of boredom. Another illustration of this behavior pattern is the Walter Mitty person who is constantly living in a fantasy instead of attending to the world around him.

This passive-aggressive behavior is an indication that a person is disgusted with the circumstances around him. Rather than being honest with anger, the daydreamer prefers to be insulting by drifting off into a world all his own. He is clearly communicating that he wants to have nothing to do with anyone else. His own fantasy life is more important than the needs of those around him. This is a stubborn way of demanding that people leave him alone.

Laziness

Once a man came into my counseling office specifically wanting to work through his problem of laziness. It was not unusual for this man to go to bed early in the evening and sleep for fourteen hours. When he was awake, whether at home or on the job, he would try to do as little work as possible. He put more energy into avoiding people who might ask him to do something than he actually put into his responsibilities. This man was truly dedicated to his lifestyle of laziness.

As we explored the relationships (both past and present) he had with his family, it became apparent why he was so lazy. All his life people expected him to perform up to a certain standard. He was constantly reminded to do his chores or to study hard. He was afraid to openly express his irritation even though this bossiness bothered him. Laziness seemed to be his most effective tool to fight back with. He sincerely hoped that people would eventually conclude that he couldn't be counted on. That way he could live life his own way.

Anger is virtually always at the root of laziness. If you don't believe it, try to get a lazy person to do something for you and then be prepared for a lot of grumbling. People who engage in this behavior are rebelling against expectations and responsibilities. Somewhere along the line they have felt cheated, misused, or misunderstood. But they have been afraid to let their feelings be known for fear of punishment or condemnation.

Hypochondria

A hypochondriac is someone who experiences one minor illness or pain after another. Usually the physical discomfort is real, at least in the hypochondriac's mind. People who use this form of behavior usually fall into one of two categories: they are sick in order to gain attention, or they are sick in order to avoid people. In either case, these people are reluctant to face emotions in a normal manner. I have never worked professionally with a hypochondriac who was not also hostile.

One of the reasons people become hypochondriacs is that they have been made to feel guilty whenever they speak out in an assertive manner. They learn that in order to be able to say anything negative, one needs to have a good excuse. That's where illness comes in. People who have physical aches and pains are not expected to be in good moods. In fact, they will assume that by being ill they have a legitimate reason for complaining. What a perfect cover for someone who feels grumpy! By being stricken with one small problem after another, these people can control others in fine fashion. Their sickness gives them a built-in excuse for avoiding any requests that they don't want to honor. They can avoid spending time with people they do not like. And they can get away with making all kinds of selfish demands. Rather than risking direct confrontation, these people can release their anger in a seemingly more socially acceptable fashion.

Silent, passive anger is so deadly because the object of the anger is not given a chance to share in working through problems. Silent anger is specifically designed to kill any type of personal exchange. People who use passive-aggressive behavior are pessimists. They assume that if their true feelings are made known, they will be rejected.

In the short run, passive-aggressive behavior seems to have some real advantages, namely, the sidestepping of negative feelings. However, in the long run the disadvantages begin to pile up. Because the anger is not properly dealt with, it is likely that it will remain inside until either a blowup or an emotional breakdown occurs.

PART Four

Getting Anger Under Control

13

The Importance of Personal Security

The way a person handles anger is ultimately a reflection of that person's self-image. In fact, nearly all emotional responses are in some way an offshoot of the way people feel about themselves. As an example, a person who continually pouts and broods in a passive-aggressive way may feel weak and fragile, indicating a self-image that is bruised or unsure. The person who is aggressive and loud may need to cover up feelings of insecurity by appearing bold and unbeatable. However, these are generalizations, and it would take more insight into a person to make an accurate judgment.

But it is safe to say that the more people fall into anger, the less secure they tend to feel about themselves. Keep in mind that the anger referred to here is not just the type expressed by yelling. It also includes expressions such as the silent treatment, sarcasm, and criticism. The number of ways anger can be expressed is limited only by the creativity (or is it conniving?) of the person who gets angry.

One thought we want to hold on to is that anger is not all bad. It does have its positive function. After all, when people are angry, they usually are trying to take a stand for themselves and their convictions. Anger is a way of trying to seek out proper respect or attention. ("I want to be treated fairly. I want you to consider me as a person of worth.") In its most positive form, anger is strength in that its very basis is a desire to be understood and respected as a person.

But the problem with people who chronically use anger is that they do not really seem to believe that they are worthwhile. If they did, why would they continue to insist (with anger) that they be treated properly? A secure person recognizes that there will be times when other people will do things wrong or say things that are inappropriate. But it will not be a total surprise. This person recognizes that, as imperfect sinners, others cannot always be expected to be perfect (nice as that would be). Chronically angry people, on the other hand, seem shocked and personally insulted that anyone could possibly do or feel or say anything that could be interpreted as an insult.

If you look closely, you will find that there is a hidden grandiosity in people who have problems with anger. That is, they seem to want people to always treat them with dignity and respect (which is normal), but there is disbelief that anyone could dare find fault in them, be in a bad mood in their presence, or simply have faults of their own. It is as though the angry person is communicating, "What are you doing with problems, and why do you happen to choose to act ugly toward me?" The frustration certainly is understandable. No one likes to be on the receiving end of contemptible treatment. Yet this is reality.

The secure person is a realist. These people keep in mind that other people will be unpredictable. They learn not to have high expectations for people (even the best of people), yet they hope for the best. They recognize that if others are in a foul mood, that is their problem. And if someone wants to give them an insult, they do not necessarily feel obliged to accept it. Their philosophy is that chronic anger usually produces headaches and tight stomach muscles, which can be avoided when they decide to maintain their composure in the midst of turmoil.

This is not to say that secure people never get angry. What is necessary to emphasize is that their anger is spent on important matters and not wasted on trivial ones. They recognize that it is irresponsible to simply let the world go by with all its injustice and never take a stand. Certainly secure people have convictions. They are wise enough to discern when it is proper to take a stand, and when it is senseless or unprofitable. This points out that there is a delicate art to deciding when to pursue anger and when to simply let it go.

There are two rules of thumb to follow in deciding when to use anger.

1. Personal convictions are being violated by someone else.
2. It is the responsible thing to express convictions.

Note that anger is an act of responsibility. There may be times when a person's convictions have been violated, but to express anger would be irresponsible. For example, individuals sometimes come into my counseling office and proceed to tell me (before they even get to know me) that they do not believe that counseling ever does anyone any good. Imagine that! If I wanted, I could accept such a statement as a direct personal insult. Indeed, it goes against my convictions. But rather than getting angry, I usually remind myself that this person is looking for an argument, which he will not get from me. My assumption is that if this person is open to new experiences, in time he can change his mind and perhaps think differently. For me to get angry would be irresponsible because it would probably give that person the "proof" that will allow him to keep his idea.

But there are plenty of times when expressing anger is the correct thing to do, and in fact, it could be irresponsible to not get angry. I am thinking of a man whose wife repeatedly sabotaged the rules he had laid out for their children. This made him angry. He realized that she was violating his conviction regarding their joint childrearing task and that he needed to stand up for himself. He also realized that he needed to confront his wife, so they could come to an agreement regarding their role as parents.

From these examples it is evident that anger itself is neither intrinsically right nor wrong. It is when and how anger is used that makes it right or wrong. The secure person will use discretion, while the insecure person will not act according to a well thought-out game plan. The insecure person is too concerned with self to do that. Notice the different characteristics that secure and insecure people use.

Secure	Insecure
The person is rational.	The person is controlled by feelings.
Discrimination is used.	Emotions are expressed erratically.
Anger is responsible, purposeful.	Anger serves no constructive purpose. It is irresponsible.
The person tries to be a realist.	The person is an idealist.
The person has proper humility.	The person has hidden grandiosity.
The person recognizes that the world is imperfect.	The person will not accept that people are going to be imperfect.

Security rests in relation-   Security rests in relationship with God.   ship with people.

Probably the most difficult concept that people struggle with in learning to handle anger is that it can be controlled with a rational mental process. They complain that they cannot make unwanted feelings of anger go away simply by putting their minds to work. And, in part, they have a good point. That is, emotions cannot be turned on or off like a light switch. But they can be controlled and monitored.

After all, included in the mind that God gave each of us is a will. Each mentally competent human being has the willpower to make decisions regarding how he will handle his life and emotions. The problem today is that people tend to look to *other* people to do things right before they feel that they can get a grip on their emotions. This is wrong, and this is dangerous. Rather than waiting for other people to "get their acts together," the most responsible thing a person can do is to take the initiative to get one's life in order even if others do not do their fair share.

I will admit, deciding to get a mental grip on anger is one of those things that is easier said than done. However, it is safe to make the assumption that the mind is more powerful and more stable than all the emotions. If not, we all are in trouble!

The greatest way a person can have a solid, unshakable sense of security is to know the full love of God. Too often, people get so caught up in their problems and in their personal relationships that they forget to develop their relationship with Him. When we get a solid grasp on the love given to us in the life and death of Jesus Christ, the feeling of security is enormous.

Many people have a hard time accepting the fact that God loves them. Perhaps a spouse has been selfish and inconsiderate. Or maybe they had parents who had difficulty showing love. They may know other Christians who in their weakness are insensitive and seemingly unconcerned. They are influenced by these human frailties. But God is not human. When you witness the weaknesses of people, you can allow that to serve as a glorious reminder that there is One who will never act in such a way. He is always perfect. He is always consistent.

The more a person becomes absorbed in the value and worth that God places on every single individual, the more capable that person can feel to separate himself from the negative messages and ugly reality that the world often offers. Each person can know this for a fact because of what the Bible tells us in passages such as Ephesians 2:8–9 and John 3:16–17. Because we know the Word of God is perfect and can be trusted, it is important in our search to control anger to look to the Scriptures for guidance. In the next chapters, we will pursue this.

14

The Bible and Anger

$\mathbb{T}$he Bible has much to say about the use of anger. It mentions both of the types of anger described in chapter 5. There is responsible anger (assertiveness) that is used in helping one another live proper lives. And there is irresponsible anger (aggressiveness) that is motivated by the sin in our lives.

In order to determine how we are to best use anger, we need first to consider what God's goal is for each of us. Certainly He did not create humans just so we could have material possessions (though He wants us to enjoy them). And neither did He create us just so we could fall in love with someone and have a happy family life (though this, too, is something He wants us to enjoy). The primary reason God created mankind was so we could have the pleasure of knowing His love. This is shown throughout the pages of the Scriptures. God created people as creatures who are capable of both giving and receiving love. This, in part, is what is meant by being created in the image of God.

However, from the very beginning man made mistakes. We did things that seemingly indicated that we didn't care about God. But did God turn His back on us? On the contrary. The more we sinned, the more He drew close to us. In fact, He loves us so much that He gave us His Son,

Jesus, to pay the punishment of our sins so we can have eternal life with Him. Without doubt, our overwhelming goal in life is to come to know this love that God has for us. It is indeed overwhelming.

Our second goal in life, after we have discovered God's love, is to live our lives in such a way that others can come to know God's love as a result of our witness. This is why it is so important to learn to use anger in a proper manner. In its perfect form, anger is an emotional gift given to humans by God to help us in our interactions with one another. If we can use anger as a building instrument we will be using it to the benefit of God's kingdom. However, we have one main roadblock, our sin nature, that we must guard against.

Let's look at what the Bible has to say about anger. First, anger-provoking, difficult situations can be looked upon as an opportunity to grow: "Consider it all joy, my brethren, when you encounter various trials; knowing that the testing of your faith produces endurance" (James 1:2–3).

Many people are so preoccupied about conflicts (*sometimes* understandably) that they see nothing constructive in them. Indeed, conflict is not pleasant. It can cause some people to become tense, depressed, disillusioned, and irritable. And, to be truthful, we know that it is usually difficult to handle conflict in a skilled manner. There often is a panic reaction, with aggressive anger surfacing in one form or another. We all have witnessed what poorly-managed conflict can do. No wonder so many people fear conflict. This, though, can give us extra incentive to go to the Scriptures to learn how to use anger properly. From this passage we know that when we do, we can learn positive traits such as endurance.

Many people are confused about what the Bible says about anger. For example, they will read certain verses and decide there is a contradiction in what we are instructed to do.

"Be angry, and yet do not sin; do not let the sun go down on your anger . . ." (Eph. 4:26).

"Let all bitterness and wrath and anger and clamor and slander be put away from you, along with all malice" (Eph. 4:31).

In one verse we are given the "go-ahead" to be angry. But just a few verses later we are told to put anger aside. Some people will read this and conclude that the Bible is simply a book of contradictions and that we can't believe what it says. Not so. In Ephesians 4 we are introduced to the two types of anger, assertive and aggressive. Unfortunately, because of the translation from the original Greek to English, we do not get the full picture this passage paints.

In plain English we are told: "Stand up for your convictions when you know you are right, but be tactful and considerate. Don't express anger in such a way that it causes you to harbor feelings such as bitterness and condemnation. And get over your anger instead of holding on to it too long." In other words, when we as Christians decide to work at having a loving, caring lifestyle, it does not mean that we are always supposed to swallow our anger. We have a responsibility to speak up! But we are to speak in a constructive rather than a condescending way. This is partly what the writer to the Ephesians had in mind when he said, ". . . speaking the truth in love, we are to grow up in all aspects into Him . . ." (Eph. 4:15).

But let's proceed cautiously with our review of anger. We know that we have permission to be angry and that anger is a responsibility. But in our eagerness to be confrontive we are capable of overdoing. We need first to examine some of the cautions given to us regarding anger.

Anger Gets the Yellow Light

"Let all bitterness and wrath and anger and clamor and slander be put away from you, along with all malice" (Eph. 4:31).

There is an old saying that we are judged by the company we keep. Often anger keeps company with a pretty rough crowd. Look at the accompanying characteristics mentioned in this one verse: bitterness, wrath, clamor, slander, and malice. What company! We know that there is a fine line between looking out for our best interests and being selfish. What starts out as correct anger can easily turn sour when it gets mixed up with our sin nature. (This is why we are told to keep anger on a short time limit.) When our sin nature becomes involved, automatically other wrong emotions come, too. Anger expressed wrongly can be obnoxious. We know from this verse that other ugly traits are ready, willing, and able to "tag along" and turn anger into a destructive emotion.

"You have heard that the ancients were told, 'You shall not commit murder,' and 'whosoever commits murder shall be liable to the court;' but I say to you that every one who is angry with his brother shall be guilty before the court" (Matt. 5:21–22).

This passage is not meant (as some assume it to be) as a condemnation of all anger. In speaking these words, Jesus meant to warn His listeners that none of us is incapable of the worst expression of anger, murder. The pious religious leaders of the day assumed that since they kept the rules of the church, they were righteous. But Jesus let them know that even though they had never committed the act they were still not to be puffed up, because within themselves they had what it took to become murderous people. This applies to us today. We are all capable of being scalawags. This is part of our human condition. This points to our need for divine intervention in handling our emotional problems. If we are left on our own, there is no limit to the amount of ugliness we are capable of getting involved in. This passage serves as a sobering reminder of what we as sinners are capable of doing if we give ourselves too much rein.

"Do not fret because of him who prospers in his way, Because of the man who carries out wicked schemes. Cease from anger, and forsake wrath; Do not fret, it leads only to evildoing" (Ps. 37:7–8).

This passage warns us against becoming angry for the wrong reasons. The example the psalmist uses in these verses regards a person who becomes angry because of another person's illicit gains. This type of anger (jealous anger) leads only to wrongdoing. It could result in envy, bitterness, slander, or even hatred. Too often our eyes are focused on superficial things such as the glamorous lifestyle or the elegant possessions of others. We complain that it is unfair that others should prosper beyond our own prosperity, particularly if they are con artists. Unfair as it truly is, we still have no right to condemn. Besides, what difference does it make, as far as my personal security is concerned, if others have more than I? What good does it do to blow up? Certainly anger is best saved for matters of real importance.

"But let every one be quick to hear, slow to speak, and slow to anger" (James 1:19).

When God inspired the writing of the Scriptures He knew that quick anger is a serious problem for us. This explains why we are advised to be slow to anger. Too many of us exhibit the trait called "popping off at the mouth." We can be so quick to become offended and to speak out that our outbursts of anger are harmful, since we usually don't take the time to view the full picture. We become so absorbed in ourselves that we do not listen for objective facts. A person who is quick to anger is almost always a poor listener. And a person who is a good listener is not quick to anger. The writer, James, is strongly suggesting that most anger could be avoided if we each determined to live consistently within our Christian principles.

"An angry man stirs up strife, And a hot-tempered man abounds in transgression" (Prov. 29:22).

Simply put, people given to chronic anger are likely to be troublemakers and are prone to do things in a thoughtless manner. When people become angry their thoughts are moving at ninety miles per minute. Impulses race through their minds in a disjointed fashion. Angry people are likely to not think through matters in a rational way. It is easy to get caught up in spur-of-the-moment wrongdoings. No wonder we are warned to be careful in the way we use our anger. It can be like matches in the hands of a seven-year-old child—dangerous.

As a result of the verses pointed out here (along with countless other verses not mentioned), we can conclude that anger is to be used quite carefully. The Scriptures continually remind us that as imperfect humans we are capable, even likely, to take a normal emotion such as anger and make something irresponsible out of it. Dynamite can be used for constructive purposes, such as clearing land for the building of roads. But we all know how destructive it can be when it gets into the wrong hands. Such is the case with anger. Anyone who physically handles dynamite is very cautious. Likewise, anyone who uses anger is advised to be cautious.

After reading passages of Scripture that instruct us to be conservative in the use of anger, some people go too far. They try to *never* be angry. Remember, that is not our goal. Let's not throw out the good with the bad. We know that Jesus Christ became angry. If we examine His use of anger, perhaps we can learn from it.

Jesus and Anger

The best known and most widely referred-to illustration of Jesus' anger is when He encountered the money-changers in the temple (Mark 11:15–17). Jesus had gone to Jerusalem the week before His death to observe the Jewish Passover. When He entered the temple He found profiteers selling animals, supposedly so the worshipers could make proper sacrifices to God. In truth, these men intended to make money. Naturally, Jesus held the strong conviction that these people's behavior was a high insult to God. Not only were they wrong in their behavior, but also they had the audacity to do their cheating at the temple!

Jesus' anger was strong and forceful. He let the money-changers know in no uncertain terms they were to leave. To get their attention He turned over their tables and physically drove them out! No doubt He knew that quiet diplomacy would not work with these people. Therefore He chose a harsh means to communicate His message. (Notice how infrequently He chose to use this method of communication.)

Certainly the anger expressed in this instance could be called assertive anger. Jesus was holding firmly to His beliefs about the sanctity of the temple and He would not tolerate such irreverence to God. The thing that distinguishes this anger from aggressive anger is that it had a constructive conclusion. I doubt if the moneychangers were quick to set up shop again. Also, Jesus was able to express His anger without harboring feelings of hatred and bitterness. We are not told that after this incident He went away sulking and plotting to do evil. In fact, He was able to continue with the business of the day—teaching and ministering to the people. It is truly amazing to imagine a man having an angry outburst, being perfectly righteous, and carrying on afterward in a responsible manner. Let's say it's not human.

Another illustration of Jesus' anger is found in Mark 3:1–6. In this case, Jesus had gone to a synagogue on the Sabbath and was met there by a man with a withered hand. The religious leaders were keeping their eye on Him, wondering if He would break one of their laws by healing the man on the Sabbath. (Heaven forbid!) Jesus sensed their nature and it stirred his emotion. We are told, "And he looked around at them with anger, *grieved* at their hardness of heart, and said to the man, 'Stretch out your hand'" (Mark 3:5, RSV; italics added). In spite of their disapproval of Him, He did what He knew to be correct.

Notice the emotion that accompanied Jesus' anger. He felt grief. With His anger He was hurting for these people. He had such a love, such a concern for these men that it broke His heart to witness their cold nature. His anger, as always, was born not of a sense of malice but of a sense of love. He stood firm in His conviction that the healing power of God takes priority over a silly manmade rule. His anger was His way of communicating that He would not be intimidated by foolish rituals. He had only one intention—to demonstrate His love.

A third illustration of the anger of Jesus is recorded in Luke 9:51–56. It came at a time when Jesus and His twelve disciples were going on a journey from Galilee to Jerusalem. It was the custom of the Jews traveling between Galilee and Jerusalem to go around the region of Samaria, even though it was directly en route. This was due to a long-standing hatred the Jews had for the Samaritans, since the Samaritans were considered to be of mixed blood. However, Jesus thought this custom silly, as He had no hesitation in traveling through the unfriendly country. In Samaria, Jesus had attempted to stay over in one of the towns, but the people did not receive Him. His request was turned down. This insulted the disciples and their reaction was typical of humans. "They said, 'Lord, do you want us to bid fire down from heaven and consume them?'" (Luke 9:54, RSV). Of course, Jesus was not interested in their petty style of vengeance. Instead of getting angry at the Samaritans for turning Him down, Jesus became angry with the disciples: "But he turned and rebuked them" (Luke 9:55, RSV).

This illustration provides a stark contrast between aggressive anger and assertive anger. The disciples' anger was definitely motivated by spite and vengeance. It had no useful function. In their expression of anger their only aim was to prove a sense of superiority. Clearly Jesus did not appreciate this attitude. Because His nature is love, He was ashamed of the hatred they demonstrated. Jesus' anger toward His disciples was used to communicate a deep truth. He wanted them to learn that vengeance did not have a rightful place in their lives. Their goal in life was to be the same as His. That is, He wanted them to be messengers of God's love.

Through these three illustrations of anger expressed by Jesus we can learn some important guidelines.

1. Anger is appropriate when it is meant as an expression of unwavering truth founded in the love of God.
2. Anger can be expressed directly and to the point.
3. Anger is not the same thing as hatred and vengeance. It should be constructive, not destructive.

It is gratifying to know that Jesus Christ felt angry from time to time. That teaches us that anger is not a wrong emotion. Each of us has the task to try to follow the principles for expressing anger that are spelled out in the Scriptures. We have the perfect example to follow in Jesus Christ.

15

Love Comes First

Most people who have trouble with anger would admit that they would like very much to be more composed and levelheaded in their lifestyles. This would be consistent with biblical teachings about human relationships. One example after another in the Scripture points toward the idea of kindness and warmth in our interactions. A lifestyle of contentment is high on the list of priorities for Christians.

This does not mean that Christians are supposed to be spineless, passive sissies. Not at all. There is nothing passive or weak about having a caring, tender disposition. Unfortunately, through generations of brainwashing, our society has been led to believe that only women should be gentle and kind. I hope, though, that people today can see through this idea. Both women and men have a responsibility to demonstrate love in their everyday lives. No matter how powerful or how brilliant a person may be, if love is not a part of one's life, then life is a failure. This was in Paul's mind when he wrote, "If I speak with the tongues of men and of angels, but do not have love, I have become a noisy gong or a clanging cymbal. And if I have the gift of prophecy, and know all mysteries and all knowledge; and if I have all faith, so as to remove mountains, but do not have love, I am nothing" (I Cor. 13:1-2).

Many people read this passage of Scripture and will agree that love indeed is needed in their lives. But they often have one nagging question that keeps haunting them: "Exactly what is love?" They hear that we are to love one another, but when they are asked to explain what love means, they cannot define it.

Before a person is able to live a lifestyle dedicated to calm, evenhanded thinking, it would be helpful to know what love is. Following are some of the key characteristics of this emotion.

Love Is Unconditional Acceptance

It is easy to state that people need to accept one another as they are. But it is a lot harder to accept someone when he is exhibiting flaws that directly affect one's life. One teen-ager put it this way: "I can accept people the way they are as long as they don't bother me."

Our human tendency is to accept one another with conditions attached. All people have their own needs and interests that they want to fulfill. When someone poses a potential problem to those needs, he is a menace. And who wants to fool with menaces? It is human nature, then, to look out for oneself and to scorn anyone who gets in the way. But notice how this is exactly opposite to God's nature.

"But God demonstrates His own love toward us, in that while we were yet sinners, Christ died for us" (Rom. 5:8).

Every human being alive has done things that are displeasing to God. In our behaviors, we have let Him know that even though He desires good behavior from us, we'll do whatever we please. All people have exhibited a defiant nature against the will of God. If He wanted, He could give mankind the same rejection in return. He could tell us that there is no way He will allow anyone who defies Him to experience His forgiveness. But that's not God's style. God has let mankind know that in spite of our sinful ways, he will take us just as we are. His love is too great to be erased by sin. We are instructed, "Therefore you are to be perfect, as your heavenly Father is perfect" (Matt. 5:48). In other words, God has set the standard and it is our task to work toward that standard. Even if we can find many *traits* in a person that are unacceptable, there is still the possibility of accepting the *person* just as He does.

Love Is Understanding

Many people get angry with one another only to find out later that the anger was the result of a misunderstanding. Learning to have an understanding spirit can do a great deal to bring calmness to personal relationships. Understanding is something that is given away. It is a gift.

An understanding attitude can be in direct contrast to a condescending, provoked attitude. Too often people see flaws and weaknesses in other people, and their response is anything but understanding. Many tend to look at the faults in others with a condemning, judgmental heart. One of the favorite games people love to play is the inferiority-superiority game. It is easier to get caught up in the game of one-upmanship than to have an understanding heart. There is less giving and therefore less of a chance to be vulnerable.

Understanding is made possible by empathy. Empathy is the ability to feel another person's experience as though it were one's own experience. This is an ability all people have, but not all people use. Everyone knows what it is like to feel hurt, or sad, or frustrated, or lonely. But the angry person would like to pretend that it is not right for someone else to have those feelings. It spoils his hopes for a perfect existence in which everything works according to plan.

The greatest act of empathy was committed by God through Jesus Christ. God saw that His people were sorely afflicted because of the sin of the world. He was so moved that He decided to take on the hardships of a man in the person of Jesus. As a human, Jesus knew the hurts of personal rejection and sorrow. Because He allowed Himself to be fully human, people were able to sense the understanding He had for their lives. He communicated to them that He knew them through and through. Those whose hearts were open to this care were able to experience the sense of peace that comes from knowing that God truly cares for them.

As Christians, we each have the responsibility of demonstrating the same kind of understanding that Jesus Christ had. Chances are, the more people try to place themselves in the positions of those around them, the less prone they will be to anger.

Love Is Forgiving

Too much anger exists because of an unforgiving spirit. People are skilled at keeping score in their interactions. They hold grudges. They try to induce guilt in one another. Yet some of these same people have the audacity to approach God for His forgiveness. One of the great traits of a Christian is that he can put mistakes in the past and move progressively forward.

Jesus once got into a discussion with His disciples about forgiveness. Peter thought he was demonstrating a generous heart by suggesting that one should forgive a brother seven times (rather than the customary three times). But Jesus replied, "I do not say to you seven times, but seventy times seven" (Matt. 18:22, RSV). In other words, forgiveness is a process that never stops. Each man and woman can be thankful that God sets no quotas for the number of times a person can be forgiven.

Speaking for myself, I know that I would have no hope if God had limited His forgiveness for me. The more we appreciate the forgiveness of God, the more we will be willing to forgive one another.

Love Recognizes That We All Are Equal

I have already mentioned that one of the reasons anger gets out of hand is because of feelings of inferiority and superiority. However, the truth is, there is no such thing as an inferior or a superior person. We are all the same.

Many people have a hard time grasping this concept. They witness the differing skills and capabilities of people and conclude that some people are obviously better than others. Nothing could be further from the truth. Different does not mean better or worse. It simply means different. It is utterly astounding to recognize the obsession we humans have for labeling one another as better or worse, smarter or dumber, sophisticated or unrefined.

This is one area that is very clear in scriptural instruction. The Bible makes no distinction between one sinner and the next. It states, "For all have sinned and fall short of the glory of God" (Rom. 3:23). It doesn't say anything about some people sinning more and some sinning less. It is plain and simple. We all are equally guilty before God.

Many times in my counseling office I have heard two types of comments.

"I think I could be pretty loving if I could only believe that I am as good as other people."

"I think I could be pretty loving if others just weren't so rotten." (Translated: "I'm better than they are.")

Both of these styles of thinking are wrong. Likewise, both of these styles of thinking make a person susceptible to expressions of aggressive anger. It is correct to recognize that while we all are different, we all are the same.

Love Is Patient

In the love chapter (I Cor. 13:4–7) of the Bible there is a description of the characteristics of love. At the top of the list is patience. It is no coincidence that patience precedes the other traits mentioned. After all, if a person is impatient, it is difficult to be kind, humble, not jealous, not rude, and so forth.

Patience is something that goes against basic human nature. Because of sin, each person has the tendency to be selfish. It is common for a person to worry more about what will happen to himself than to have concern for others. Consequently, when we encounter trying circumstances our reaction is to hope and even insist that things work out in the best way possible as soon as possible.

Since love involves denying self, a loving person will be concerned with the welfare of others. Love does not have to have its own way and it can tolerate weaknesses and differences in others. By patiently working with potential problem situations a person can reduce the opportunities for anger.

Love Is Realistic

One of the reasons people have a difficult time being loving is that they assume love is an idealistic, pie-in-the-sky way of feeling. They are probably confusing love with romance or infatuation. The type of "love" that is based on idealistic thinking usually ends in bitter disappointment.

It is realistic to admit that differences will occur among people. But the angry individual does not allow for variety. He wants people to behave just as he prescribes. In his sane moments, he will admit that it truly is unrealistic to expect others to perform to his specifications. But once he allows his emotions to get control of his life, all reasoning goes out the window. Even though he knows logically that he is wrong, he lets anger rather than reason be his guide.

God always intended for realistic thinking (not emotions) to be the guiding force in one's life. Being created in the image of God means that each person has the ability to choose his own avenues in life. While love is a feeling, it is also a style of decisionmaking. Any person can choose to respond to others in whatever way he sees fit. This means that before erupting in an emotional outburst it is possible to decide whether one will be angry or caring in a given circumstance.

16

Steps Toward a Life of Composure

Once love becomes part of a person's life, it is then possible to go forward with the steps needed to insure a lifestyle of composure. By being composed, a person is in control of his emotions rather than having the emotions in control of him. He can make rational decisions regarding how anger will be handled. He is able to determine whether his anger is being expressed as004assertively or aggressively. A composed person is not necessarily free from anger. That is not even the goal. Rather, a composed person lives life in as constructive a way as possible. Emotions are very much a part of this lifestyle. They add the spice to life.

The greatest example of composure is found in the life of Christ just before His death on the cross. We know that on the night of His arrest, Jesus experienced some deep emotions (Luke 22:39–46). Apparently He felt emotionally weakened, because He was in need of an angel to give Him strength. We also know that He was in great agony. The sweat from His brow was as drops of blood. In addition, we know that He felt disappointment because His disciples fell asleep when He needed them by His side. Yet in the midst of such an emotional experience, Jesus never lost His composure. And from further accounts of His mock trial, we know that He experienced total composure.

One of the most embarrassing experiences for any human being is for that person to lose a grip on himself in the midst of an emotional experience, particularly when the emotion is anger. Things can be said or done that are totally out of character. After the experience is over, there can be a feeling of shame and guilt.

In order to keep these types of experiences from happening, a person needs to have a plan of action for his life. It is best to think things out in advance so a person can make use of his God-given ability to control his emotions. That way, our emotions will work for us, not against us.

Set Your Priorities in Life

Angry people usually have the goal to make other people live up to their expectations. They may say that their first priority is to be a good husband, a good wife, or a good Christian. But through their behavior, they are showing what they really want.

The age-old question of the philosophers is: "What is life all about?" Christians have the perfect answer. To live is to know God. Therefore, the first priority is to get to know God and to become absorbed in His love. The second priority is a direct result from following the first. That is, we are to do our best to help others know the love of God. The rest of a person's priorities will all hinge on these two. An angry person needs to ask himself, "Is my anger helping me to meet these two priorities in life?" If the anger is then considered consistent with these goals, express it. If it is not, release it.

Develop a Sense of Self-worth

One's emotional life will always hinge on his self-image. People who have a poor self-image are guaranteed to have problems with anger. They will have either open, biting anger or passive-aggressive anger. As mentioned earlier in the book, depression and anxiety can be included as expressions of anger. Usually when people have problems with controlling anger, it is a signal that their self-image is maladjusted. More than likely, there is too much dependence on others to make these people feel good. Since no person is perfect, no person is able to give another a complete sense of self-worth.

Self-worth is based on the love given to us by God. When God sees our sinful ways, He does not reject us (as people are likely to do). He loves us even more. Every human being is like a precious jewel to God. He wishes harm on no one. He has made the ultimate sacrifice, Jesus Christ, to demonstrate the hugeness of His love. A person who gains a deep appreciation for this awesome love can be assured of a positive self-image. If God is for us, that's enough!

Have a Servant's Heart

Once a person knows the love of God, he can focus on giving that love to others. This in turn can guarantee that his emotional needs will be met, since we receive by giving. Most angry people are too concerned with what they are going to get from others. They worry about getting recognition, appreciation, and rewards. There is nothing necessarily wrong with these things. But most want too much, or they want it now. Impatience gets the best of them.

Rather than waiting for people to give to them, these people would do better to initiate the giving. For example, I've talked with many angry people who think that no one tries to show understanding toward them. However, the opposite is usually also true. That is, these people aren't being very understanding themselves. If they would give, they might receive. This doesn't mean that we should give in order to receive. Even if we receive nothing, giving is still worthwhile. It can lead to a feeling of contentment.

Recognize Your Own Limitations

Angry people can be very demanding. Very often they demand things of others that they are not even capable of doing themselves. For example, one husband demanded that his wife always be patient with him, even when he made mistakes. Yet he admitted that he was not always perfect in that area. By admitting his own weakness, he was able to ease up on his frequent use of anger.

Very often in anger there is a certain sense of grandiosity. It is as though the angry person has the right to get angry because he has completely conquered all his problems. On the other hand, it is very rare to find a man who knows true humility and yet explodes in constant anger. The more a person recognizes his own imperfections, the more careful he will be in expressing anger. When he does express anger, he tries to express it as constructively as if he were on the receiving end.

Accept Imperfection in Others

This step is one of those that is easy to say, but hard to do. To be honest, some people can be so hard to live with that it is difficult to have an accepting attitude. But accepting someone does not mean condoning his behavior. It is possible to love a person without liking what he does.

Family members have particular trouble with accepting the weaknesses in one another. After all, they can't just excuse themselves and leave each time a weakness shows in a loved one. Sometimes there is nowhere to go. They often feel trapped with someone who has wrong behaviors! In situations like this, it takes a huge amount of determination to accept the one who is hard to live with. This is when it is vitally important to remind oneself that the goal in life is not to make others fit a certain mold. If other people are going to make changes, they need to feel the freedom to make their own choices. Knowing they have acceptance from loved ones can be a positive motivator. This may not always work, but it is preferable to a life of constant haggling and frustration.

Don't Put All Your Eggs in One Basket

There is no one human being who can give another human everything he needs. Many people have had a complete emotional collapse because of one person (maybe two) who has let them down. Anyone who allows his emotional stability to hang by a single thread is asking for trouble. One woman let her entire life get wrapped up in the life of her husband. But one day he died unexpectedly, and she went into a deep depression that lasted for years. This example is typical of how many people try to gain satisfaction from one person. It's great, *if* it can last forever.

Many angry outbursts are due to the problem of putting too much dependence on one person. If that one person does not live correctly, pandemonium erupts! The most secure people are those who have several support systems at once. That way, if there is a lull or a disturbance in one, there is a cushion to fall back on.

Let Others Love You

Countless people have uttered the complaint, "You just don't love me." A few of these people are correct, but most of them suffer from poor perception. What they really are saying is, "You don't love me the way I want you to love me." If the love is not exactly on their terms they want to have nothing to do with it. It's "my way or no way."

Each person has a different background. That means that each person has a different set of experiences to draw upon. What may be unloving to some may be loving to others. For example, I know one woman whose husband would poke her when he felt loving and attracted to her. She would angrily snap at him each time he did this, so he stopped doing it. But to the wife's dismay, he got discouraged and was reluctant to show any kind of love. Certainly the wife was right in saying something to her husband about his annoying habit, but she overreacted.

It takes as much skill to know how to receive love as it does to give it. To be realistic, some people are not very good at giving love. But just because they do not show love in a perfect way doesn't mean it should be rejected. I have a young niece who likes to give me a kiss when she says good-by. A kiss to her means that she puts her mouth next to my cheek. She is not exactly what you would call a good kisser. But considering her motive and her limitation, I welcome her with open arms anyway. It's not how she does it, but that she does it.

Be Your Own Person

Recall that anger is a person's way of standing up for his own beliefs and convictions. The reason so many people have trouble with anger is that they want others to confirm them. They look to others to give an agreeing nod

or an affirmative word. When they don't get it, they feel
cheated. Anger is their way of expressing immature hurt.

Adults have the ability to live independent lives. That
is, they can choose to feel good about themselves regardless of what others say, think, or do. This is consistent
with the thought that every person needs to be responsible
for himself. God has given each person a sense of willpower. Determination to live a responsible life is the real
key to success.

Too often, people allow their circumstances to control
them because they feel weak. They allow their feelings
rather than willpower to be the guide. There are times
when it is appropriate to determine to press ahead in
spite of what the feelings say. This doesn't mean that
feelings are useless and should be ignored. It means that
people would do best to use some rational thinking before
letting their feelings go helter-skelter. This will enable
persons to rise above negative circumstances and be what
they choose to be.

Do Favors for Yourself

No one was ever intended to have to live the life of a
martyr. Too often anger directed at other people is incorrect, since the angry person is doing nothing to help
himself. All people need to give themselves permission to
be "selfish." That is, there are times when no one knows
what you need better than you do. So rather than waiting
on someone else to do a favor for you, do one for yourself!
It can be a lot of fun.

One ten-year-old boy told me that when he has a particularly bad day, he takes a dollar from his piggy bank
and goes to the store around the corner to play video
games. This is his gift to himself. There is a calculated
risk in giving permission to do favors for oneself. It can
always be overdone so that it becomes a pattern of real

selfishness. But when done properly and moderately, it can help a person come to a sense of satisfaction, knowing he can positively affect his moods.

Learn the Art of Being Tactful

Many people place themselves in volatile situations because of a loose tongue. Too often people who have good intentions get themselves in difficulties because they say things the wrong way. It is sometimes hard to allow for the fact that communication involves two people. Those two people each have separate needs and separate feelings. For communication to be successful, the needs of both need to be considered.

Also, honesty is not always the best policy. For instance, a husband says to his wife, "I never did like your family." He may be very truthful, but he probably is not very considerate. Since love is the guide in communications with people, it makes sense that people should take extra precautions to say things in as loving a way as possible.

It would be nice to proclaim that all a person has to do to have a happy life is to follow these few easy steps for living. But that would be naive. All people are imperfect. This means that no one person will ever completely be able to live a totally pure life. But we can keep on trying! Even though we won't reach perfection in this life, we still have the responsibility to get as close to it as possible.

17

How to Argue Fairly

$\mathbb{B}$y now it should be pretty obvious that there are at least 1,001 ways to botch the expression of anger. It can be repressed. It can be expressed in hit-and-run techniques. It can take on manipulative passive-aggressive traits. Unfortunately, the majority of the times when people become angry, they usually resort to some sinister way of handling anger.

But remember, anger is not necessarily bad. It can be a powerful building tool when it is used correctly. It is a necessary emotion to give people an inner boost to make a firm stand for their convictions. In that sense, it has a useful function. With proper use of anger, people can move toward open, constructive communication.

Because we live in an imperfect world, anger will always be a part of life. That is, people will always have a need to stand up firmly to wrongs. The way people learn to express anger will determine whether the world will become even more imperfect or more refined. Let's hope there will be enough responsible people who will sense the need to find a constructive style of give and take in expressing anger.

Learning to express anger is a skill that needs constant practice. It is not something that automatically comes to a person. Consequently, it can be helpful to refine the skill of expressing anger by following some rules of personal interaction. Listed are twelve steps for communicating anger properly.

1. Learn to discriminate essential from nonessential problems. One of the main reasons anger gets so out of hand is that people argue about the wrong things. There is a children's story about a couple that lived in an isolated part of the forest. One evening about bedtime these two people got into an argument about who would shut and bar the door. Both were so stubborn that each vowed not to move or speak until the other person shut and barred the door. In the meantime, some thieves came to the house and had a heyday. They didn't understand why the couple refused to move or speak. Fortunately a valiant prince came along at the end of the story to save the day.

In real life, many people get caught in similar stubborn struggles. They will argue and fume endlessly about minor problems. Many people admit that once their arguments were finished, they forgot what the original problem was! And to make matters worse, in real life there are no valiant princes to come along to rescue them!

We only have one life. So there is no need to spend time fussing and fuming over minor problems. When you get angry, make sure it is over something that is worth being angry about!

2. When problems arise, confront them as soon as possible. Once you have decided that you have a genuine reason for being angry, go ahead and do something about it. You know the old joke about fishermen's tales: The more time that has passed since they caught the fish, the bigger it was. The same is true with anger. The longer a person waits to get it off his chest, the bigger the problem becomes. Memory seems to have a way of exaggerating things.

Once an angering thought gets pushed into the memory, it grows. In my counseling practice, I see people who are angry about events that happened years ago. Sometimes the feelings are very intense. But as these people begin to look at things objectively, they usually admit that things were not as bad as they thought. If they had confronted the feelings when they occurred, they could have been spared years and years of misery.

3. When you are angry, stick to the subject. When you express anger there will always be the risk of not being taken seriously. This threatens some people. In order to make sure that their point is well made, they like to have a little extra ammunition. A wife who is angry with her husband for being sloppy may decide to also remind him that he forgot to pick up bread on the way home from work. To add a little extra zest to her outrage, she may also let him know that she's angry at him for not taking her out to dinner in a long time. She adds that she never did like the way he acts when he is around his friends. And then she'll criticize him for skipping church last Sunday.

You can imagine the response of the husband. He either will find the nearest hole to shut himself into or he will fight back. The wife may have some legitimate complaints, but enough is enough! Hopscotching from one subject to another rarely accomplishes anything positive. The emotions are like an electrical outlet. It is dangerous to be overloaded.

4. Be honest in expressing your feelings. Too often arguments are simply exchanges of intellectual philosophies. People say to one another: "I think you should . . ." or, "My theory is that. . . ." You can go to any college campus to discuss all the theories you want. With friends and family members, though, feelings need to be expressed. "I feel angry when we don't get to see our friends together." "I am hurt when you ignore me." By expressing feelings, you have something pertinent and specific to deal with.

To be sure, there are risks in expressing feelings. Some people find a lack of acceptance on the part of others when feelings are expressed. Others recognize the immaturity or inappropriateness of their feelings when they are being openly discussed. Yet most of the times when feelings are properly expressed, the advantages far outweigh the disadvantages.

5. Avoid terms of exaggeration. This suggestion is consistent with the idea of sticking to the subject. When they are angry, people tend to make statements such as, "You are always late" or, "You never show any consideration." Words such as "always" and "never" are unnecessary. They have a way of getting the subject off the track.

Angry people also tend to exaggerate in the way they describe their problems. "Today has been so unbelievably horrible, it is absolutely the worst day of the century!" Statements like that only make matters worse. Usually the problems people get angry about are not as bad as they seem. This isn't to say that most problems are insignificant. (That would be exaggerating to the other extreme.) Try to think and speak in middle-of-the-road terms.

6. Refrain from character assassination. Because insulted feelings often accompany anger, many people have the tendency to want to strike back. If they are going to feel hurt, they feel they may as well drag the other person into the mud, too. It is easy to recognize the harm in a statement such as "Looking at you makes me believe in evolution—you're nothing but a baboon." It would be rare to find someone who would have a kind reaction to this opinion.

7. Listen to understand. Communication is a two-way street. It involves not only speaking but also listening. Anger, in its pure form, is supposed to be a building instrument. It is not very constructive to simply unload

your feelings without being responsive to the reaction of the other person.

Listening involves more than just the act of hearing. It involves understanding and concern. Too often, in periods of anger, people "hear" what they want to hear without making the effort to try to understand what is being said and felt. One college student put it this way: "I feel lonely and empty, but when my parents are angry they just think I'm lazy. They don't try to understand." It is only when two people begin to understand what is behind one another's feelings that depth and meaning become part of the relationship.

8. Don't ask loaded questions. It is almost humorous to listen to some of the circular talk that goes on in an argument. Very often one person starts out with a loaded question and gets a loaded question in return.

> **Him:** "What makes you think you're smart enough to tell me what I ought to be doing?"
>
> **Her:** "Don't you think I have the right to tell you when you're wrong?"
>
> **Him:** "Just what kind of a fool do you think I am?"
>
> **Her:** "I don't know, what kind of fool are you?"

Loaded questions have one purpose—to trap the other person. And everyone knows that when someone feels trapped, he is not going to communicate from the best frame of mind. In order to be successful in expressing anger, it is necessary to create an atmosphere of understanding. There is a good rule of thumb to go by in expressing anger: Avoid asking questions unless you want constructive information. Try to make statements instead.

9. Give yourself a time limit. Many people can hang on to anger for unbelievably long periods of time. I talked with one woman who was angry with her husband about a mistake he had made twenty years earlier. And when

she mentioned this to him, she literally could talk for hours and hours about it. Long-term anger is very destructive. It only grows worse as time goes on. It can be likened to an acid slowly eating away a person's internal organs.

In arguments, it is best to keep the discussion to a limited period of time. Usually it takes less than ten minutes to get the facts and the issues out in the open. Add a few more minutes to share feelings and show understanding, and the argument should be over. After thirty minutes, most of what is being said is repetitive. If an angry interchange lasts much longer than a half hour, then one of two things is probably happening: the anger is being poorly communicated, perhaps vaguely or abrasively, or someone isn't listening very well. Once the argument is settled, go on about the business of daily living. Don't keep going back to it.

10. Keep a positive attitude. Some people are frightened half to death of anger. They see it as one of the worst sins imaginable. This fear is understandable if anger is used for the wrong purposes. But anger itself is neither right nor wrong. The way it is handled determines that.

One young bride was told by an old family friend that she and her husband had never argued in their thirty years of marriage. The bride was gullible enough to think that this was desirable, so she set her goal to never be angry with her husband. Imagine the sense of failure she must have felt whenever she started to feel angry! Certainly it is healthy to work toward building a pleasant atmosphere around loved ones. But a person is asking for trouble if he never expects anger.

Anger is as destructive or as constructive as a person will allow it to be. If a person has a negative attitude about anger, it will be bad. But if a person keeps an accepting, positive attitude toward it, it can be seen for the normal emotion that it is.

11. Be tactful about when and where you choose to express your anger. I know of one man who would rarely correct his children unless their playmates were around. For some reason, he felt the need to prove his power at these times. Naturally the children resented him for it.

The circumstances in which people choose to express anger can tell a lot about their real motivations. A person who seems to have a habit of getting angry in public could be motivated by factors such as group sympathy, group pressure, or chicken-heartedness (there's safety in numbers). A person who chooses to express anger in private at an appropriate time probably is letting love lead the way.

12. Winning is not the goal! The goal in expressing anger is to create an opportunity for growth. Many people have improved themselves considerably by learning to understand their own anger and the anger of others. But nine times out of ten they have improved only because the climate was right. Arguing through intimidation is guaranteed to make someone lose. And if one person loses, all lose.

A key factor to help you detect whether you are trying to win an argument is to examine how strongly you are trying to be convincing. The word *convince* comes from a Latin word meaning "to conquer." Anyone who is trying to make a convincing argument is trying to conquer. Chances are, the argument will end in frustration.

The real winners are those who can learn to control their anger. Anger, like any other emotion, is too unpredictable to allow it to be in control. There is no telling what kind of roller-coaster ride one's emotions can take. The reason God gave each person a mind is so we each can think through our emotions. If your anger is not being handled in the way you want, it is a signal that your thoughts need to be re-evaluated. Slow down long enough to examine the real reasons for your anger. Make anger your ally, not your enemy!